RETRO
GRAPHICS

★ ★ ★ ★ ★ ★ ★

SendPoints

SendPoints

EDITED & PUBLISHED BY SendPoints Publishing Co., Ltd.
PUBLISHER: Lin Gengli
PUBLISHING DIRECTOR: Lin Shijian
CHIEF EDITOR: Lin Shijian
EXECUTIVE EDITOR: Zhang Yu
EXECUTIVE ART EDITOR: Ho Waikin
PROOFREADING: Tang Yuqing   Luo Yanmei

REGISTERED ADDRESS: Room 15A Block 9 Tsui Chuk Garden, Wong Tai Sin, Kowloon, Hong Kong
TEL: +852-35832323 / **FAX:** +852-35832448
OFFICE ADDRESS: 7F, 9th Anning Street, Jinshazhou, Baiyun District, Guangzhou, China
TEL: +86-20-89095121 / **FAX:** +86-20-89095206
BEIJING OFFICE: Room 107, Floor 1, Xiyingfang Alley, Ande Road, Dongcheng District, Beijing, China
TEL: +86-10-84139071 / **FAX:** +86-10-84139071
SHANGHAI OFFICE: Room 307, Building 1, Hong Qiang Creative Zhabei District, Shanghai, China
TEL: +86-21-63523469 / **FAX:** +86-21-63523469

SALES MANAGER: Sissi
TEL: +86-20-81007895
EMAIL: overseas01@sendpoints.cn
WEBSITE: www.sendpoints.cn / www.spbooks.cn

ISBN 978-988-77572-6-9

CONTENTS

There is a German word that does not have an English equivalent, that is, *zeitgeist*. It means the spirit of the time, and refers to the cultural trends and aesthetic tastes that are characteristic of a particular period of time in history. Yet the nature of graphic design, combined with its connection with the social, political, and economic life of its culture, enables it to more closely express the zeitgeist of an epoch than many other forms of human expression.

Since ancient times, people have been searching for ways to visualise ideas and concepts, to store knowledge in graphic form, and to convey information in the most effective way. Over the course of history, these needs have been filled by various people including scribes, illuminators, printers, and artists, who have subtly caught the zeitgeist of the time and skillfully recorded the aesthetic appeal of a given era. These precious records turn out to be a vast treasure trove of inspiration for designers. Moreover, the classic elements in graphic design have been employed by designers unfailingly. On one hand, these classic elements evoke the nostalgia in people and remind them of the good old days. On the other hand, what exactly make these elements classic attributes to their long-lasting worth and timeless quality.

When we seek to record the past, we do so from the vantage point of our own time. The heritage of Classicism and Neo-classicism propels us to reprise the venerable aesthetic rooted in simplicity, proportion, symmetry, and decorum. The exuberant Baroque and Rococo style offers us a glimpse of drama and luxury. Medieval

Letterforms, romanticism, and decorativeness characterise the Victorian style, which demonstrates variety and intricacy in graphic design. Indeed, the design style of the Victorian era is an eclectic one, which shows signs of precision of ancient Greek, magnificence and holiness of the Middle Ages, elegance of the Renaissance, grandeur of the Baroque style and sophistication of the Rococo style. The Arts and Crafts movement advocates traditional craftsmanship by using drawings from nature and simplicity of form. It often uses medieval, romantic, or folk styles of decoration, which renders a lively and refreshing artistic effect. Art Nouveau is another decorative style that has garnered a place in the history of graphic design. Vine tendrils, flowers such as rose and lily, birds, and the female form are frequent motifs from which an organic plantlike line is adapted. In addition, the art influence from the East such as Japan and China has also provided graphic designers with fresh sources of inspiration. Female beauties, scenes from history and folk tales, travel scenes and landscapes, flora and fauna, all these elements have greatly enriched the decorative patterns.

The constant innovation of modern graphic design and the improvement of people's aesthetic sensibilities have demanded a higher level of taste and a deeper level of cultural connotation in designs. A better understanding of the past will surely enable us to continue a cultural legacy of beautiful form and effective communication. It is a nod to the classic, a tribute to the good old days, and a homage to the rich historical and cultural heritage.

THE EVOLUTION OF GRAPHIC STYLES

The nature of graphic design, combined with its connection with the social, political, and economic life of its culture, enables it to more closely express the zeitgeist of an epoch than many other forms of human expression.

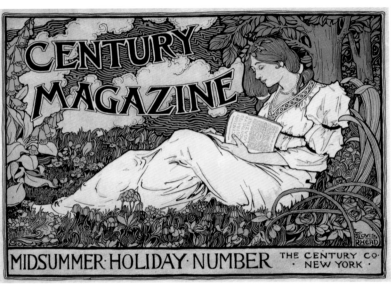

Louis Rhead, promotional poster for *The Century Magazine*, 1894

Randolph Caldecott, illustration from *Hey Diddle Diddle and Baby Bunting*, 1882

The Victorian Style

With the turmoil and anxiety caused by the first industrial revolution, a sense of nostalgia seemed to spread into the English society. A fondness for the medieval Gothic style of architecture, ornament and lettering had gained popularity. In the graphic area, the Victorian style embodies a flood of colourful printed images featuring children, maidens, flowers, and puppies which are all exquisite and delicate with elaborate borders and lettering.

Key Figures: Frederick Walker, Randolph Caldecott (Britain); Louis Prang, Louis Rhead, Harper & Brothers (America)

William Morris, text page from *The Works of Geoffrey Chaucer*, 1896

Selwyn Image, title page to *The Century Guild Hobby Horse*, 1884

The Arts & Crafts Movement

Dissatisfied by the influx of tasteless goods brought by the industrial revolution, a group of designers led by William Morris advocated a revival of traditional handicrafts. They carried out a movement with the aim to unite art/design with craft. Drawing inspiration from medieval arts, naturalism and oriental decorative arts, it is quite different from the extravagant and superfluous decoration of the Victorian style. It pursues simple forms, with inspiration coming from the botanical world. A case in point is Morris's pattern designs featuring curvy, organic lines and a natural style. Moreover, the movement also serves as a landmark in fine book design. The Kelmscott Press founded by Morris, with its idea of treating books as art objects, brought a revival of Gothic types as well as a flood of beautiful books with visual references from medieval incunabula books. In the United States, the Arts and Crafts movement also has its fair share of significance in graphic design. Designers such as Bruce Rogers and Frederic W. Goudy have helped the movement flourish in their country, whose designs pay more attention to orderliness and solemnness.

Key Figures: John Ruskin, William Morris, Bruce Rogers, Walter Crane, Arthur H. Mackmurdo, Selwyn Image, Herbert P. Horne

Alphonse Mucha, poster for 'Job' cigarette paper, 1896

Peter Behrens, *The Kiss*, 1898

Art Nouveau

Characterised by its use of sinuous lines and "whiplash" curves and its inspiration from the natural world, Art Nouveau has a major influence on graphic work and illustration. Additionally, it has drawn upon elements of Japanese art. Ukiyo-e, in particular, enjoys a profound influence on designers with its calligraphic line drawing, abstraction and simplification of the nature, flat colours and decorative patterns. The style was most popular in Europe, but its influence was global and had different names as it was spread and gained its localised characteristics. For instance, it is known as Sezessionstil ("Secession style") in Austria, Jugendstil in Germany, and the "Glasgow style" in the United Kingdom. Though known with different guises, there are some general features that are indicative of the form. The unfolding of Art Nouveau's dynamic, undulating, and flowing lines can be interpreted as a metaphor for the freedom and release sought by its practitioners and admirers from the weight of artistic tradition.

Koloman Moser, poster for the 13th Vienna Secession exhibition, 1902

Margaret Macdonald, Frances Macdonald and J. Herbert McNair, poster for the Glasgow Institute of the Fine Arts, 1895

The Glasgow School

The Scottish branch of Art Nouveau.

Key Figures:
Charles Rennie Mackintosh,
Margaret MacDonald,
Frances MacDonald,
J. Herbert McNair

The Vienna Secession

A branch of Art Nouveau in Vienna, Austria.

Key Figures:
Gustave Klimt,
Josef Hoffmann,
Koloman Moser

The German Jugendstil Movement

A branch of Art Nouveau in Germany.

Key Figures:
Otto Eckmann,
Peter Behrens

⚠ Fernand Léger, *The City*, 1919

Cubism

Cubism is a highly influential visual arts style of the early 20th century that was initiated principally by Spanish painter Pablo Picasso and French painter Georges Braque. Influenced by post-impressionist painter Paul Cézanne, Picasso created a series of works depicting the human figure in an abstract way. With the chiseled geometric planes, multi-perspective way of depicting and chaotic colours, the works voiced a revolt against the European Renaissance tradition of pictorial art. In Cubist artwork, objects are broken up, analyzed and resembled in an abstract form and are depicted from a multitude of viewpoints. Moreover, along with Braque, Picasso introduced collages and papierscolles into their work with things like paper, wood piece or grit.

Key Figures: Pablo Picasso, Georges Braque, Fernand Léger

Fortunato Depero, New Futurist Theater Company poster, 1924

★ THE EVOLUTION OF GRAPHIC STYLES ★

Futurism

In 1909, a manifesto of Futurism was declared by the Italian poet Filippo Tommaso Marinetti in *Le Figaro*, in which Filippo celebrated the machine age, technology, speed, urban modernity and even the war with great enthusiasm. Futuristic painters are fond of employing lines and colours to depict a series of overlapping shapes and intertwining layers, as well as using wavy lines and straight lines to depict light and sound, so as to express the impression of people in speedy motion. With regard to graphic design, Futurism is mainly reflected in the design of a multitude of poems and propaganda materials.

Key Figures: Filippo Marinetti, Fortunato Depero, Guillaume Apollinaire

⚠ Marcel Duchamp, *Fountain*, 1917 (Photography by Alfred Stieglitz)

Dada

Painting a mustache on Mona Lisa's face, naming a porcelain urinal "Fountain" and submitting it to the Society of Independent Artists as an artwork for exhibition were all done by French painter and sculptor Marcel Duchamp, who was also one of the most influential spokesmen of Dada. By placing an attitude of irony toward art, Dada's practitioners, including poets, painters and musicians were creating all sorts of noise and nonsense. With its absurd and willful visual form, Dada voiced the horrors of World War I, as well as an assault on a society which had already lost its humanistic spirit.

Key Figures: Tristan Tzara, John Heartfield, Marcel Duchamp, Kurt Schwitters

Giorgio de Chirico, *The Disquieting Muses*

Surrealism

Growing out of Dada, Surrealism was named by the French poet, André Breton, in his 1924 *Manifeste du Surréalisme*. Breton imbued Surrealism with words such as dreams, rebellion and the subconscious, drawing inspiration from Freud's exploration of intuition, dreams, and the unconscious realm. The Surrealist artists believed that the revelation of the power of personal imagination could be found on the street and in daily life. Through art creation, Surrealism sought to tap the unconscious mind and unlock the power of imagination, which remains enlightening to the creativity of modern graphic design.

Key Figures: Giorgio de Chirico, Andre Breton, Max Ernst, Joan Miró, Salvador Dali

Expressionism

Before World War I in Germany, many artists began to express subjective feelings and personal emotions through their works, with exaggerated or distorted proportion and jarring colour contrasts. One of the recurring themes is fear. The inspiration mainly came from the post-impressionist painters, Vincent van Gogh and Edvard Munch in particular. Lithographs, woodcuts and poster were considered very important media by the expressionists.

Key Figures: Käthe Schmidt Kollwitz, Wassily Kandinsky, Paul Klee

Pictorial Modernism

Plakastil（1900~1930）

In 1905, German design talent Lucian Bernhard created a poster for the match brand Priester. A pair of lonely matches alongside the blue brand name composed the whole graphic scene. The approach of using bold eye-catching lettering with flat colour shapes, simplified shapes and high visual communicative function was extremely groundbreaking at that time, which later triggered the movement called Plakastil (poster style). It soon became a dominating style for the commercial poster at that time, as well as the wartime propaganda posters.

Key Figures: Lucian Bernhard, Julius Klinger, Julius Gipkens

Post-Cubist Pictorial Modernism （1920s~1930s）

After World War I, the enthusiasm toward machine and technology was at an all-time high, which became a major theme for art and design. During this period, a group of designers began to incorporate cubism and the characteristics of Art Deco into their design. Based on the geometric shapes of cubism, with influence from the Bauhaus, De Stijl and Suprematism, a decorative geometric style began to be used in posters and pictorial designs. Meanwhile, simple geometric patterns showcasing features of the times, such as Egyptian ziggurats, sunbursts, lightning bolts and zigzags, were widely used to express both an efficient modern living and an elegant lifestyle.

Key Figures: Edward McKnight Kauffer, A. M. Cassandre, Jean Carlu, Austin Cooper, Paul Colin

Kasimir Malevich, *Suprematist Composition*, 1915

El Lissitzky, *Beat the Whites with the Red Wedge*, 1919

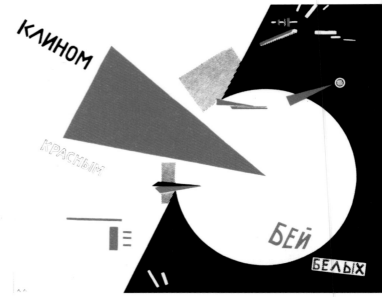

Suprematism & Constructivism

The former was founded by Russian painter Kazimir Malevich, who considered art as a spiritual activity and tried to express the purity of the art experience through the perception of colour and form. Inspired by cubism, Malevich used basic forms (square and circle in particular) and pure colour to form his painting. With his rejection of the traditional painting style of depicting real objects, a non-objective style of geometric abstraction was born. During the same period in Russia, another group called constructivism, with Vladimir Tatlin as a key figure, was holding an opposing view. Though imbued with the geometric form of cubism, it voiced a rejection of art for art's sake, advocating to jump out of traditional artistic forms and to devote to applied arts like posters and industrial designs. Constructivism is marked by the organization of abstract, geometrical elements, and combinations of different sans serif typefaces to make dynamic or visually stable forms.

Key Figures: Kasimir Malevich, El Lissitzky, Vladimir Tatlin, Aleksander Rodchenko

Piet Mondrian, *Composition II in Red, Blue, and Yellow*, 1930

★ **THE EVOLUTION OF GRAPHIC STYLES** ★

De Stijl

The Netherlands-based De Stijl movement sought to express a new Utopian ideal of spiritual harmony and order, with Dutch painters Theo van Doesburg and Piet Mondrian as the wellspring for its philosophy and visual forms. Inspired by cubism, Mondrian distilled it into a purer geometric abstraction, with the use of rectangle and square as elements, horizontal and vertical lines, primary colours of red, yellow and blue, and neutrals of black, white and grey. A visual minimalism was achieved through his works.

Key Figures: Théo van Doesburg, Piet Mondrian, Vilmos Huszar

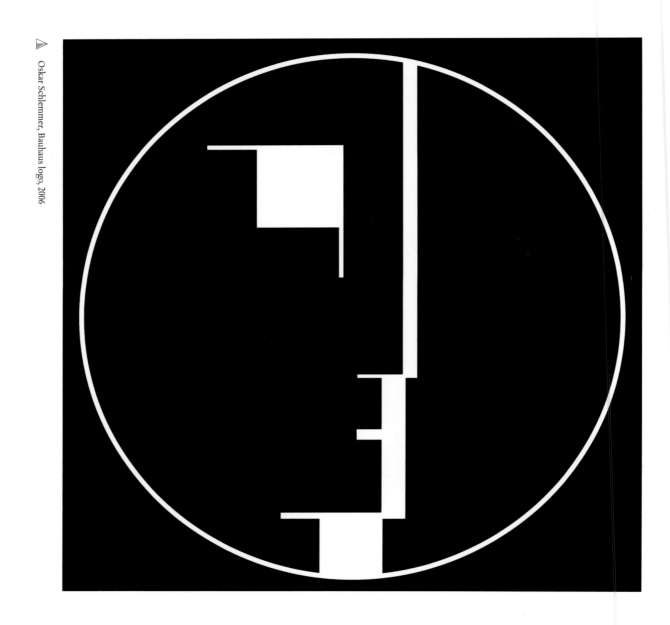

Oskar Schlemmer, Bauhaus logo, 2006

Bauhaus

In 1919, German architect Walter Gropius founded the Bauhaus School in Weimar, Germany. As the world's first school that was set for design in a real sense, Bauhaus featured a design educational system encompassing graphic, product, architectural and furniture design, thus being considered as the beginning of modern design. Derived from the Bauhaus, "design for people", "function over form", and "less is more" became the most influential design tenets during the following years of the 20th century. Geometric forms and sans-serif fonts were widely applied to the design, with minimalism as the main tone.

Key Figures: Walter Gropius, László Moholy-Nagy, Herbert Bayer, Joost Schmidt, Vassily Kandinsky

Helvetica Neue 25 Ultra Light
Helvetica Neue 35 Thin
Helvetica Neue 45 Light
Helvetica Neue 55 Roman
Helvetica Neue 65 Medium
Helvetica Neue 75 Bold
Helvetica Neue 85 Heavy
Helvetica Neue 95 Black

◁ Varying Helvetica Neue typeface weights, 2010 (Vectorised by Frozbyte)

★ THE EVOLUTION OF GRAPHIC STYLES ★

The International Typographic Style

In 1918, Swiss designer Ernst Keller joined the Zurich Kunstgewerbeschule (School of Applied Art) and became a teacher in the advertising layout course. His use of symbolic, imaginary, simplified geometric forms, and vibrant contrasting colours had inspired a group of designers including Emil Ruder and Armin Hofmann, who developed his approach and evolved it to a distinctive style with high communicative function, which was later defined as the International Typographic Style. The use of grid system, asymmetric page layout, documentary photography and sans-serif typography such as Univers and Helvetica, became the hallmarks of the style.

Key Figures: Ernst Keller, Theo Ballmer, Max Huber, Emil Ruder, Armin Hofmann, Josef Muller-Brockmann

The New York School

During the 1930s, a large amount of European designers who sought to escape from the flames of World War II came to America. With them the European modernism was initially introduced to America, which at that time, was a land of openness and freedom, like Paris of the early 20th century. All sorts of avant-garde arts were colliding with and fusing into one another, including action painting, Jazz, improvisation drama, experimental music, etc. A group of American designers began to search for a design approach, which was playful, humourous and visually dynamic, acting as a revolt against the rational and formal structure of modernist design.

Key Figures: Paul Rand, Alvin Lustig, Alex Steinweiss, Saul Bass, Cipe Pineles

H.TOMASZEWSKI '48

FOOT BALL

Henry K.Tomaszewski, football poster for the OlympicGames in London, 1948

The Conceptual Image

It is a movement emerging from Poland, America and Germany. Poland after World War II suffered from the devastation of many cultural instruments. In rebuilding the cinema, theatre and circus, posters became the most effective visual tool. Without receiving much theoretical education of western design, a group of young designers began to incorporate art approaches of the prior half-century into poster design. The unlimited and casual way fostered a unique poster design. The emphasis on concept rather than narrative expression, and the marriage of the expressiveness of art with the visual function of graphic design together created the conceptual image at that time. In the United States, the major influence was the Push Pin Style, which adopted an attitude towards visual communication openness about trying new forms and techniques.

Key Figures: Tadeusz Trepkowski, Henryk Tomaszewski, Franciszek Starowiejski, Jan Lenica, Seymour Chwast, Milton Glaser, Barry Zaid, Gunther Kiesers

Postmodernism

New Wave Typography

The initial postmodernism of graphic design was born in Switzerland in the 1960s. A group of designers strived to jump out of the structure of the International Typographic Style and infused some sort of spice and personal expression into their works. In order to get rid of the boring and rigid International Style, they embraced inconsistent letterspacing, varying typeweights within single words, and forms such as the bold stairstep.

Key Figures: Wolfgang Weingart, Dan Friedman, Willi Kunz

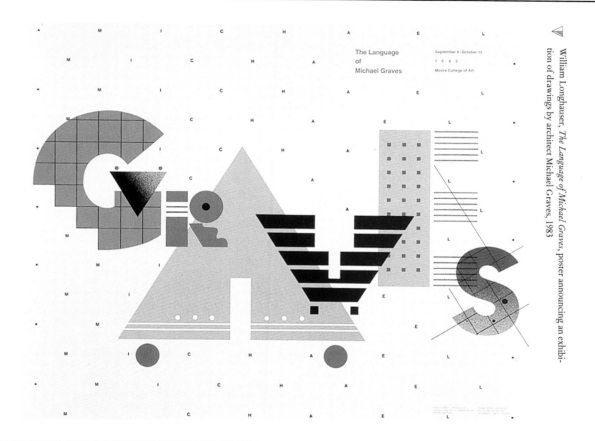

William Longhauser, *The Language of Michael Graves*, poster announcing an exhibition of drawings by architect Michael Graves, 1983

The Memphis & The Bay Area Group

The Memphis Group was founded in Milan by Italian architect and designer Ettore Sottsass in 1981. With inspiration drawn from such movements as Art Deco, Pop Art, as well as the 1950's Kitsch styles, the Memphis group created a series of colourful, bright, and exceptional pieces. Designing from one's personality, emotion and psychological needs, form not being secondary to function and creative freedom over design credos are rooted deeply in the Memphis designs, breathing a refreshing vitality into the design field. Soon after, designers from the Bay Area, San Francisco have also shifted to postmodern design. Their works shattered the rigidness and dullness of the International Style, exuding optimism and a sense of humour.

Key Figures: Ettore Sottsass, Christoph Radl, William Longhauser, Michael Vanderbyl

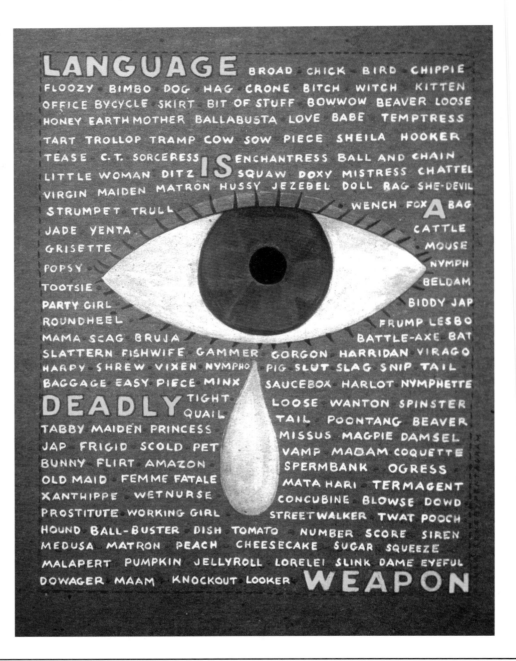

Paula Scher, "Language is a Deadly Weapon" graphic for MTV's "Free Your Mind" campaign, 1994

Retro & vernacular design

Retro style first appeared in New York, with most of its designers being the postwar generation, including Paula Scher, Louise Fili and Carin Goldberg. They drew upon the past to expand the range of design possibilities, with an interest in graphics from the early 20th century, ranging from the Victorian style to Art Nouveau and the decorative European typefaces popular during the two decades between World War I and World War II. In many of their designs, typography played a central role no less than illustration and photography, which improved the richness of the design. Similar to the New York based Retro group, the Duffy design group in Minnesota also embarked on similar design exploration, but with an American vernacular touch by drawing upon food packaging, billboards, and signage from the 1940s.

Key Figures: Paula Scher, Louise Fili, Carin Goldberg

Fred Woodward(art director), Gail Anderson(designer), Herb Ritts(photographer), *Rolling Stone* magazine, 1992

Digital Revolution in Graphic Design

During the 1980s, the first-generation Macintosh computer was launched by Apple Computer. Meanwhile, Adobe invented the PostScript programming language, and Aldus created PageMaker, a software application used for designing pages. With the birth of this series of digital technology and software, it became possible for designers to handle most of the creative process from page layout to even printing. Colour, texture, images, and typography could be handled in unprecedentedly diverse ways.

Key Figures: Susan Kare, April Graiman, Rudy Vanderlans, John Hersey, Zuzana Licko, Summer Stone, John Plunkett & Barbara Kuhr (Wired), Fred Woodward & Gail Anderson (Rolling stone), David Carson (Ray Gun)

Four Cover Designs by John Plunkett:

1.Alvin Toffler (Future Shock) Portrait, 1993

2.Illustration in Style of Antonio Prohias, 1994

3.Blank White Cover with Embossed Logo for Wired's 2nd Anniversary, 1995

4.The Greators of Doom, 1996

5.John Plunkett (concept & design) 1997. Tony Klassen (Apple illustration)

RETRO DESIGN

Retro elements are charming. They are a beautiful escape, a way to evoke nostalgia towards "the better times" of our youth or the idealized past of our ancestors. For clients retro graphics are also a way to make consumers sentimental, or to create an illusion of tradition of their product.

Vedran Klemens
Illustrator and graphic designer
Zagreb, Croatia

B eing a versatile illustrator is an advantage in a small market like Croatia. It offers me more work so that I can cover a wide range of techniques and styles. That's how I got to notice that vintage techniques and retro visuals are very much in demand lately. Art directors and clients want them as much as artists gladly deliver. Everybody seems to need them, and I think there are several reasons for that.

Borrowing inspiration from the past is always common in design, and art in general. Sometimes it is used more often than others. And I think today is one of those times when it is used more. While the world around us is changing so fast, it feels pleasant to dive back into the familiarity and warmth of the past. A reaction to the industrial revolution was a romantic escape in the medieval fantasy and arts and crafts. The same happens now, when digital revolution is plowing our landscape so intensely that it sometimes takes only a few years to dramatically change the way we communicate, work or draw.

Retro elements are charming. They are a beautiful escape, a way to evoke nostalgia towards "the better times" of our youth or the idealized past of our ancestors. For clients retro graphics are also a way to make consumers sentimental, or to create an illusion of tradition of their product. For instance, a new artisan dry cake brand would like to call for vintage graphics.

Also, one of the important reasons for retro invasion is the new digital tools that are getting increasingly powerful. They are improving quickly and becoming able to successfully imitate more and more of the traditional techniques, while at the same time making them easier to work with than they once were. One can make an illustration on a simple tablet or even cell phone that looks exactly like the one made on a scratchboard or sprayed with airbrush in the 1980s, while at the same time having all the benefits of the digital, such as layers, undos, etc. A complex illustration that looks vintage, handmade and traditional now becomes easier, faster and cheaper to make, which also means more affordable.

It's great that these retro graphics usually bring out something new. They are rarely a pure imitation, even when the artists want them to be. Simply changing the process of creation to the digital, or illustrating a contemporary subject and using the illustration in a new and unexpected context can inevitably create something modern even though the reference style may be vintage.

Summer in Zagreb — Beer Label

Designer Vedran Klemens

Ljeto u Zagrebu (Summer in Zagreb) is a summer seasonal wheat beer with orange and coriander. The illustration on a bottle label presents the nostalgic scene on the river beach in the 1930s, when it was common for Zagrebians to spend the summers there.

Favarger Chocolate

Designer Vedran Klemens

Favarger has been a Swiss chocolate manufacturer since 1826. The illustrations for a new line of chocolates Heritage revoke memory of the three founding brothers and their vintage manufacturing process. The style is inspired by the advertising illustrations from the period when the factory was founded.

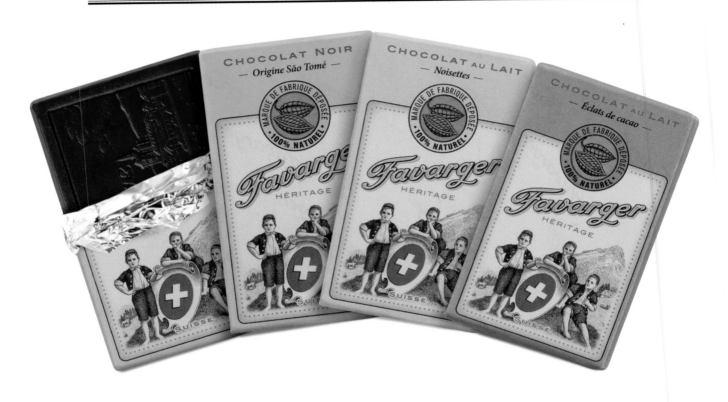

Michael Barley Photography Business Card

Studio 3 Advertising   *Designer* Tim McGrath

Designed for a photographer, each business card was made act as a mini-sleeve for a portfolio sample of his work. The texture and dimensionality of the work brings a warm and tactile feeling to the receiver, which is hard to achieve with an e-mail blast or a postcard.

Botany, "Dimming Awe, the Light is Raw"

Studio   Jared Bell

The artwork interprets Botany's eclectic musical mélange through geometric abstraction, visually referencing the Bauhaus abstractions of Anni Albers and Laszlo Moholy-Nagy, as well as the more geometric works of Ellsworth Kelly, Anne Truitt and more contemporary influences.

Split Stones

> *Studio*   Jared Bell

The idea of album "Split Stones" is about disparate halves coming together. The imagery references 1920's Surrealist and Metaphysical artists — like René Magritte or Giorgio de Chirico — who explored the curious relationship between rational thought and dreams, societal norms and bizarre hidden feelings.

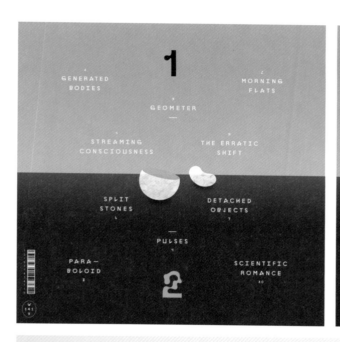

Mastiha Shop — Gift Boxes

Studio A. S. Advertising   *Designer* Kallina Kyratsouli

The island of Chios has always been the commercial crossroad of goods between East and West. Mastic, a unique product that grows exclusively in Chios, attracts elite merchants, ship owners and artists of the time. The aura of the old, cosmopolitan Chios of the 1950s and 1960s reflects the prosperity of the island with snapshots of everyday social life. With a retro mood, inspired by the people of a more romantic era, the designer created a packaging line that fits the high aesthetic standards of Mastiha Shop.

Cachaça Caboclo

Studio Estúdio Caboclo   *Designer* Ricardo Andrés & Eber Subirá

This design is a tribute to indigenous and African-Brazilian culture. The copper color reminds of Brazilian Indians' skin. Through the religion of Afro-Brazilian the designers scratched points of Umbanda. Therefore, they developed this design using those elements involved in this culture.

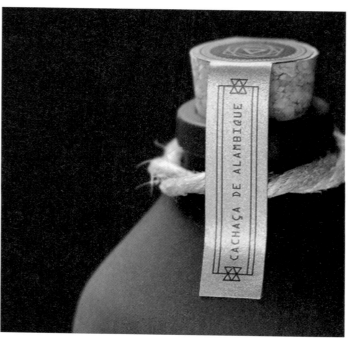

CACHAÇA DE ALAMBIQUE

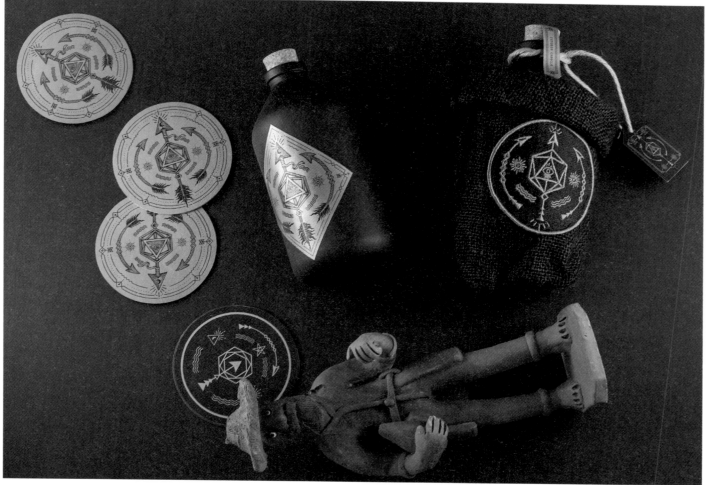

CbyB

Studio Casa Rex   *Designer* Gustavo Piqueira, Samia Jacintho & Danilo Helvadjian

This is the packaging for Brigaderia's debut chocolate range, a Brazilian confectionary store that specialises in Brigadeiro sweets. Each pack was composed through the mix of retro elements — black and white engravings — combined with simple, yet bold, coloured illustrations. A visual play of images at first might seem dissonant, but the visual contrasts come together in ludic and synesthetic visual narratives.

Forever and a Day

Designer Giada Tamborrino

The project consists of the flyer and concept design for Forever and a Day, a one-night event at Egg London. The retro theme has been chosen to enhance the name of the party — Forever. The vintage flowers embrace the letter F which is modernly shaped. It's a mix of two very different styles that gives life to a new one.

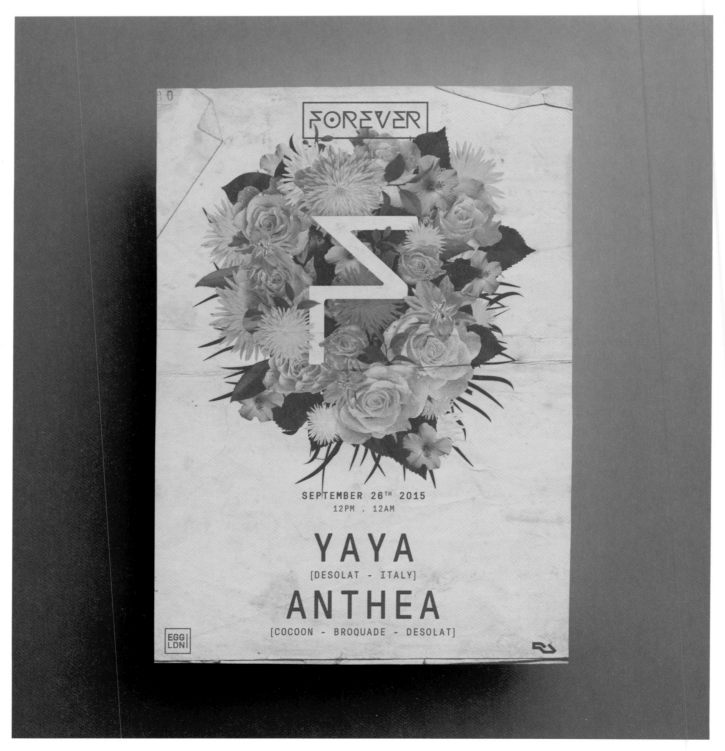

Grave

Studio Estúdio Guayabo   **Designer** Daniel Bilac & Valquiria Rabelo

In Brazilian Portuguese, "grave" is the imperative form of the verb "to engrave". It's also the name of this pioneer Brazilian company dedicated to the manufacture of engraving and printing products. The branding was designed and applied to business cards, brochures, catalogs, social media and promotional materials. Besides the logo and the color scheme, the identity is also composed by a set of public domain etchings, which are framed and remixed in the layouts.

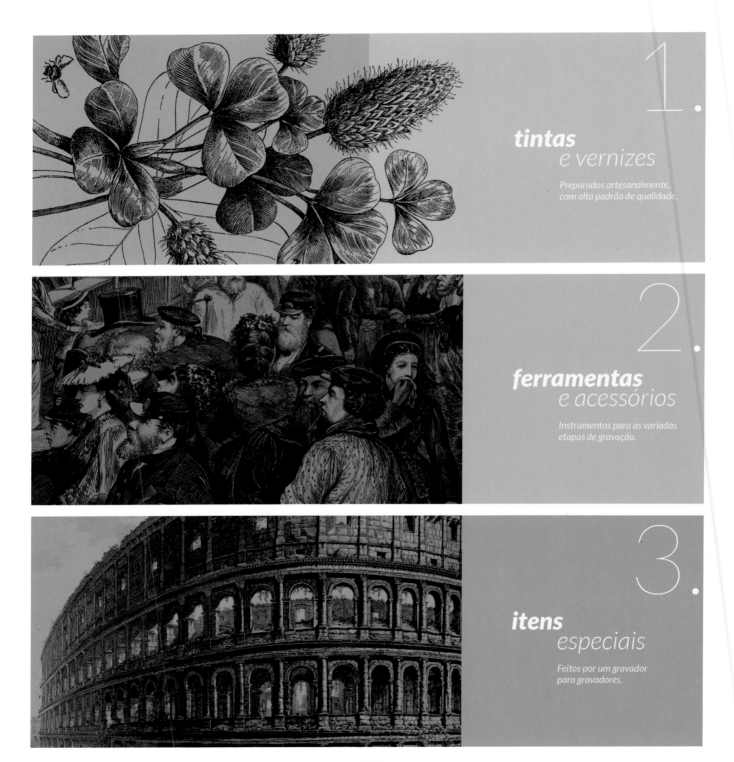

1.
tintas
e vernizes

*Preparados artesanalmente,
com alto padrão de qualidade.*

2.
ferramentas
e acessórios

*Instrumentos para as variadas
etapas de gravação.*

3.
itens
especiais

*Feitos por um gravador
para gravadores.*

Orlando Amphitheater

Designer   Dmitry "Happy End Noir" Mironov

Orlando Amphitheater at the Central Florida Fairgrounds is an open-air venue for concerts and music festivals. The main task of the project is to make an original identity system by connecting modern design and vintage emblems, illustrations and typography based on handcrafted studies. The soul of the visual style is the emblem that identifies the amphitheater in a more detailed manner.

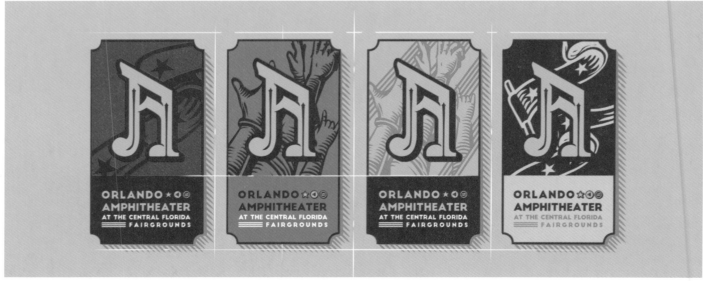

Selvática

Studio Siegenthaler & Co   **Designer** Mauricio Beltrán & Paola Avellaneda

Selvática is a brand of fruit infusions of the natural rainforest of Colombia. The designers wanted to depict the environment of Amazon rainforest in which the Acai, the Camu-Camu, the Copoazu, and the Arazá fruits grow. The illustrations show the environment in which they flourish, the animals that feed from them and how the harvest is collected.

Food Gifting Packaging Project

Designer Millie Marotta

The designer was commissioned by Marks & Spencer to produce a collection of illustrations to be used on various items of packaging across their Spring Food Gifting Ranges for 2013/2014. As the collection was to be launched in the spring time, the designer wanted to illustrate something that suggested this time of the year. Therefore, she decided to explore various plants within the artwork including flowers, buds, leaves, new shoots, grasses and ferns.

MARKS & SPENCER

ROSE
FLAVOURED
CHOCOLATE
ALMONDS

MARKS & SPENCER
All butter
STRAWBERRY
SHORTBREAD
MINI ROUNDS

MARKS & SPENCER

CARAMEL
COULIS
TRUFFLES

DELICIOUSLY CREAMY
CARAMEL COULIS
CHOCOLATE TRUFFLES

Andevine

Studio Co Partnership *Designer* Zoe Green

Andevine is a boutique wine brand created for Hunter Valley winemaker Andrew Leembruggen. As it is a debut release of Andrew's brand, it was important for the design to reflect his brand story — his Dutch ancestry and his Australian upbringing. The labels are illustrated with the national flowers of the Netherlands and Australia, creating a memorable letter A in the oil painting style of the Dutch Masters. The name Andevine is a fusion of the winemaker's first name and the very beginnings of the story, the grape vine.

Spirit No. 13 & Patented Bottle Sleeves for Safeway

Studio Stranger & Stranger

Stranger & Stranger identified 22 niches and buying occasions that might benefit from enhanced packaging and developed a patented bottle sleeve that contains everything from quotes to recipes. With the idea coming from their own No. 13 pack, they created brands in a packaging format that stands out and adds value, interest and gifting opportunities.

Semper Opera Season 13 and Season 14

Studio Fons Hickmann m23   *Designer* Raul Kokott & Susa Stefanizen

Semper Opera 2013
Fons Hickmann m23 designed the poster campaign for the Semperoper Dresden with a series of posters, flyers and books. For the poster series, designers used historical paintings and copper engravings, fragmented them and finally put them back together in a new way. The Collage was the ideal playground where they combined historical material with coloured surfaces.

Idomeneo

Wolfgang Amadeus Mozart

★ RETRO DESIGN ★

PREMIERE

29.11.2012

Aufführungen
2., 6., 10., 13. & 17.12.2012

Informationen & Karten
0351 4911 705 / semperoper.de

Semperoper
Dresden

Design Fons Hickmann m23
Gemälde Quos ego (um 1635), Peter-Paul Rubens, SLUB/Art.plast.159-1

Semper Opera 2014
Fons Hickmann m23 did it again and started the 2014 season of the Semperoper Dresden with a spectacular campaign for its premieres. It all began with Georges Bizet's *Carmen* followed by *Elektra* from Richard Strauss. In m23's design every subject got combined through cut-outs of two photographs which entered into a dynamic relationship.

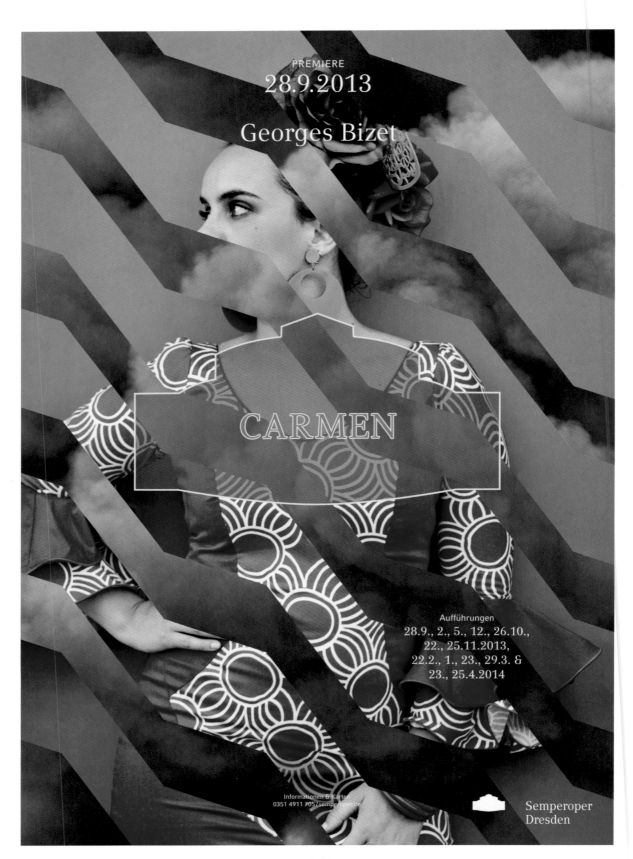

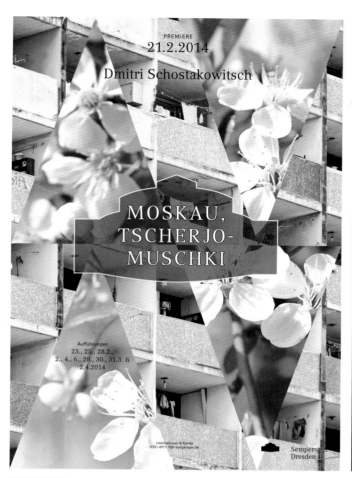

PREMIERE
21.2.2014

Dmitri Schostakowitsch

MOSKAU,
TSCHERJO-
MUSCHKI

Aufführungen
23., 25., 28.2.,
2., 4., 6., 28., 30., 31.3. &
2.4.2014

Informationen & Karten
0351 4911 705/semperoper.de

Semperoper
Dresden

PREMIERE
19.1.2014

Richard Strauss

ELEKTRA

Aufführungen
22., 25., 31.1. &
22., 29.6.2014

Informationen & Karten
0351 4911 705/semperoper.de

Semperoper
Dresden

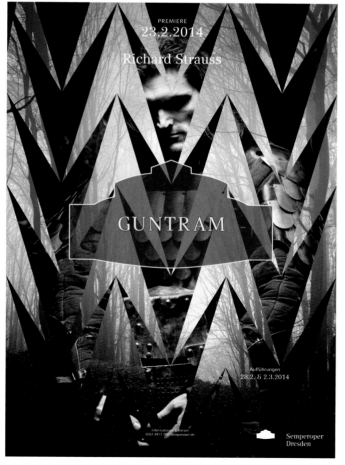

PREMIERE
23.2.2014

Richard Strauss

GUNTRAM

Aufführungen
28.2. & 2.3.2014

Informationen & Karten
0351 4911 705/semperoper.de

Semperoper
Dresden

PREMIERE
30.11.2013

Stefan Johannes Hanke

DER
TEUFEL MIT
DEN DREI
GOLDENEN HAAREN

Aufführungen
1., 4., 5., 6., 8.,
10., 11., 12.12.2013

Informationen & Karten
0351 4911 705/semperoper.de

Semperoper
Dresden

2012 Letterpress Calendar

Studio Mr cup   *Designer* Fabien Barral

For the 2012 calendar edition, the designer wanted to experiment some font works with the numbers to push the visual possibilities offered by the letterpress printing process. Each month number has its own design, based on his passion for old numbers, papers and ornaments.

Atwood Blend

Studio Chad Roberts Design   *Designer* Chad Roberts

As the result of the collaboration between Balzac's Coffee Roasters and award-winning Canadian author Margaret Atwood, the design highlights their commitment to the environment and concern for avian ecosystems. The illustration was chosen to emphasize this important aspect of the product. By combining the stunning illustration with a strong typeface, the new design has significant shelf presence that emotionally engages consumers.

★ RETRO DESIGN ★

Accents Decoration

Studio La Tortillería   *Designer* Zita Arcq & Sonia Saldaña

This project aims to highlight the meaning of an accent and its importance in different settings to create a unique space. With that in mind, the designers decided to give a face-lift to Accents Decoration's image for their sixth anniversary, marking the beginning of this new phase. The ultimate makeover is simple yet exudes a sense of sophistication with the use of black and white.

FERNANDA ULLOA

AMAZONAS 305 OTE. · COLONIA DEL VALLE
GARZA GARCÍA, NL 66220 MÉXICO
52 (81) 8356· 9558 / (81) 8335· 0321
FERNANDA@ACCENTSDECORATION.COM

WWW.ACCENTSDECORATION.COM

Basha Market on Broadway

Studio Sciencewerk Design   *Designer* Danis Sie

Basha Market is an exciting thematic bazaar, the very first thematic bazaar held in Surabaya with highly selected vendors from fashion to food and beverages. Sciencewerk designed the identity for Basha Market's first event with the theme of "Broadway". Illustration was inspired by the busy and colourful view of Broadway Street, focusing on typographic signage to create a fun, quirky environment within the event.

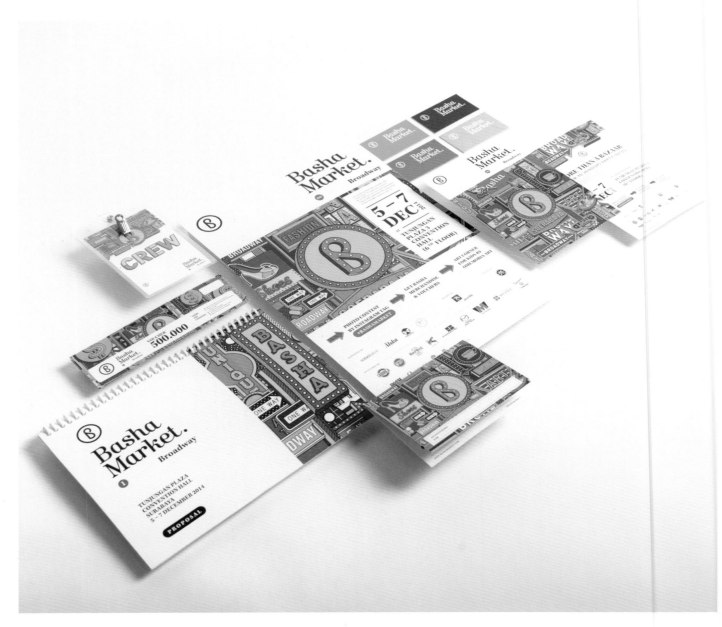

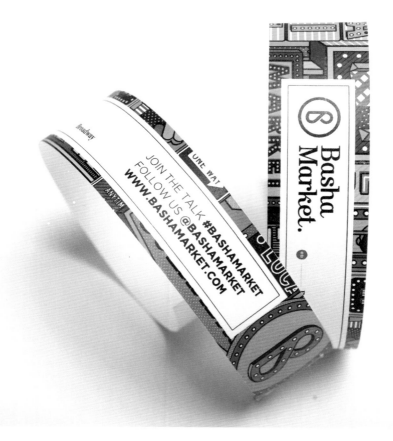

Bottura

Studio Foreign Policy Design Group   *Designer* Liquan Liew, Ella Zheng & Huinee Lim

Familiar fare passed down from "nonna" ("grandmother" in Italian) is the backbone of the cuisine at Bottura. Bottura marries nonna patterns with quintessential Italian patterns as an homage to the owner's hometown in Bologna, a city steeped in culinary tradition. The logo is a bold juxtaposition of old and new, giving Bottura a strong Italian voice. Colors are inspired by the warm hues of Bolognese food and its iconic brick roofs, forming a hearty palette.

BOTTURA

EAT
DRINK
ITALIANO

Celebrating Marriage

Studio ANONIWA *Designer* Naoto Kitaguchi

The logo featuring a leaf motif reflects a ball in an old mansion surrounded by greenery. Various forest animals were chosen as the key visuals to render an enveloping, warm atmosphere for the special day.

Risya & Nana Wedding Invitation

Designer Cempaka Surakusumah

The wedding of Icha & NANA was themed as "flower and pastel". For their wedding invitation, the designer set a tone of mint, pastel and a little bit of gold filled with flowers and leaves, giving a sweet and romantic mood. So everyone who receive the wedding invitation would feel like they receive a beautiful bouquet.

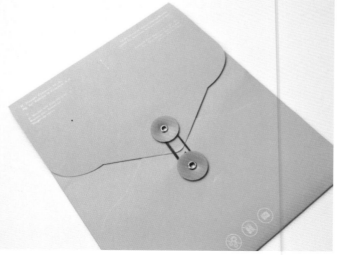

Pernikahan

ICHA & NANA

Minggu, 2 Juni 2013

8: Container Gardening Kit

Studio August Studio   *Designer* Joel Derksen

8 is a container gardening kit that unites the social elements of food, ethical and moral issues about food production and contemporary technology. The design focuses on the autumnal, cozy, and nostalgic feelings we get when we reflect upon food, combined with a contemporary sensibility.

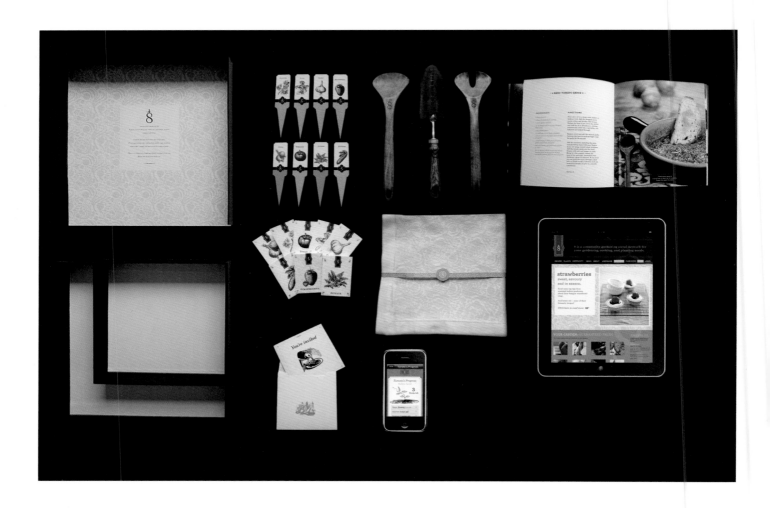

Crow's Nest

Designer Pavel Emelyanov

This corporate identity was inspired by vintage wrought-iron signs and weather vanes. Black crows are chosen for the graphic illustration because of their intelligent character. Some natural materials, textured and Kraft paper are reproduced in a vintage style while the monochrome black printing supplements warm shades of stationery.

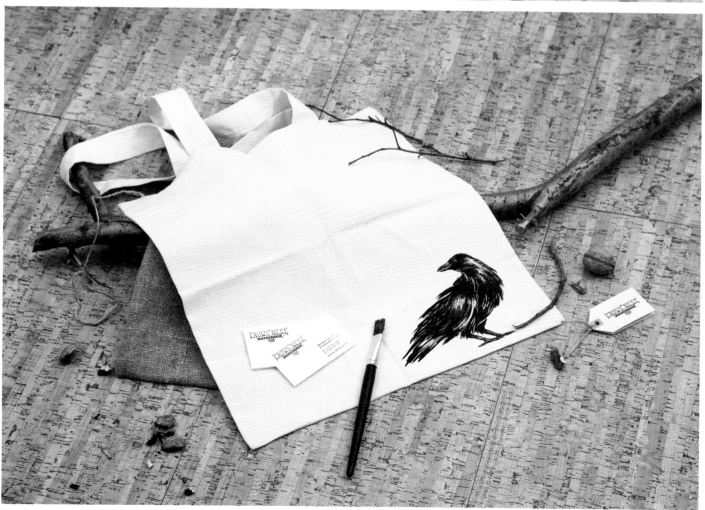

D & U Wedding Stationery

Designer Doreen Baldauf-Uhlmann

The layout of the stationery is deliberately clean and simple so that the focus is set on the lettering. The handmade letters were inspired by old typefaces on buildings, in ephemeris and from old magazines and newspapers in the 1920s-1950s. The invitation has a modern design but is printed in an old-fashioned way of letterpress.

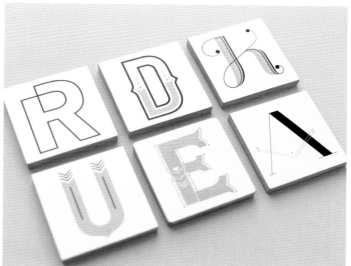

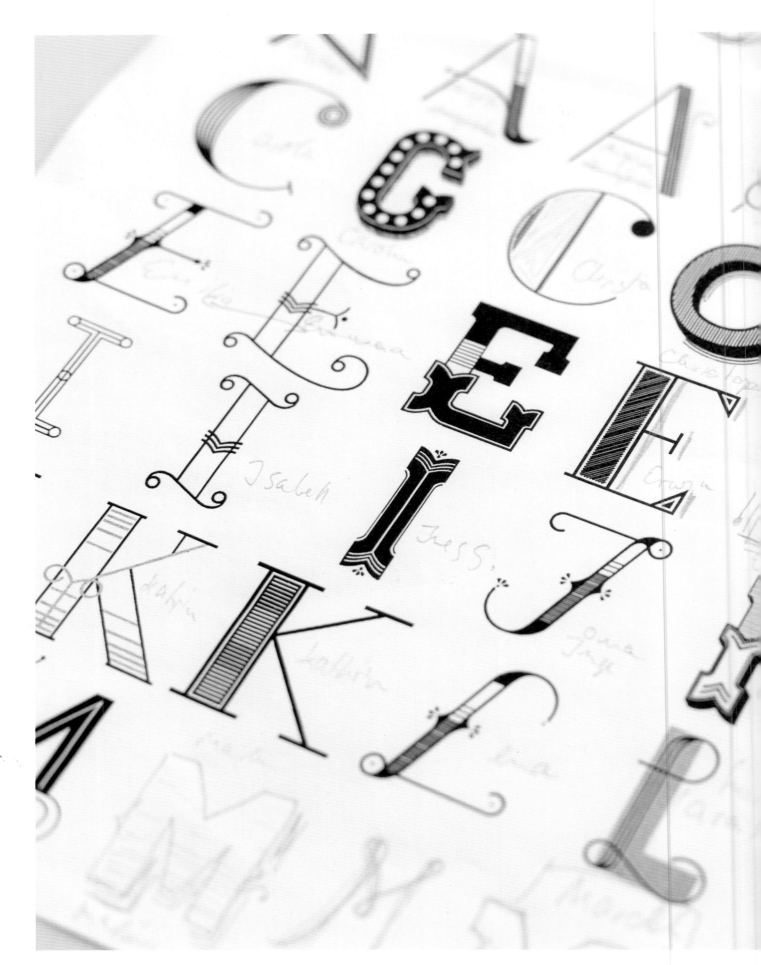

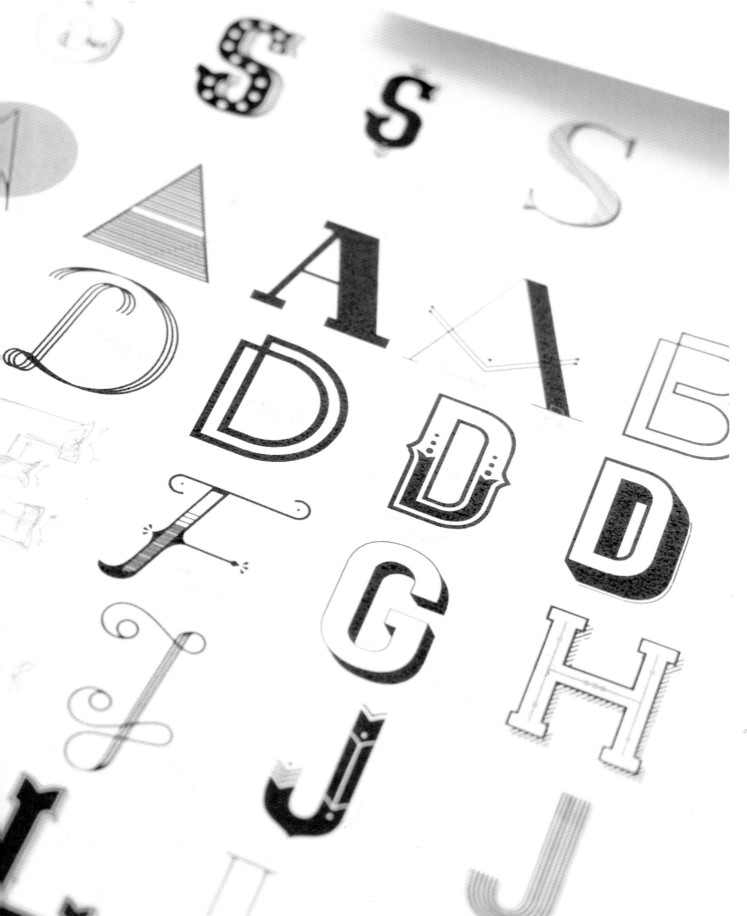

Ecoya Limited Edition Christmas 2013 Packaging

Studio Daryl Feril Studio   *Designer* Daryl Feril & Nina Richards

Ecoya Ltd. is Australia's leading eco-luxe home fragrance, bath & body brand. For this project, the designer was to create 3 different illustrations that will be used for Ecoya's Limited Edition Box Sets and a few individual packing for the holiday season. The illustrations were used as patterns for selected boxes of their products and were wrapped around the snakeskin-textured boxes. The design revolved around their French Pear and Lotus Flower candle scents. It was a burst of overlaying and intertwining flowers and foliage.

ECOYA

CARAMELISED PLUM PUDDING
NATURAL SOY FRAGRANCED CANDLE

BOTANY BAY, AUSTRALIA

ECOYA

FRESH PINE NEEDLES
NATURAL SOY FRAGRANCED CANDLE

BOTANY BAY, AUSTRALIA

Elo & Fer Wedding Invitation

Studio El Calotipo Printing Studio   *Designer* Nelson Moya & Carla Nicolás

Elo and Fer wanted to have sunflowers on their wedding invitations. Around this idea the designer aimed to create cheerful, colorful and full-of-life invitations. The use of different fonts and nature elements made their invitations reflect not only the ceremony itself but also a family party.

Elo y Fer

Os queremos invitar
a nuestra boda
que tendrá lugar, el próxi
7 de diciembre de
en la | **San Miguel**
Iglesia de | **de los Navarros** a las

Después lo celebraremos e
HOTEL PALA

VEN CÓMODO,
PORQUE SERÁ | CON UN RICO
UN DÍA LARGO | **BANQUETE** A LAS

Emmanuelle

Studio Violaine et Jérémy   *Designer* Jérémy Schneider

The name Emmanuelle is in reference to the French mythic erotic movie of the 1970s. The brief of this project was about femininity but not girly, sexiness with delicacy, sensibility with strength. The designers made long research about feminine icons, symbols, representations through many different ages, from Egyptians to modern life, and then assembled details and icons into one piece. The logo consists of a point-down triangle (women), a braid (through ages, hair has always been a seductive attribute), an apple (Eve, the first woman according to the Bible), fishnet stockings (a classic sign of erotica), the Ouroboros (eternal love) and the arrow (Cupid's arrow, the arrow of seduction).

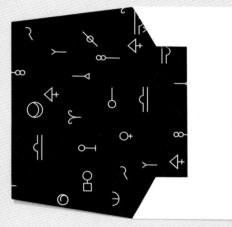

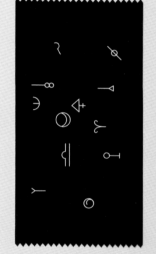

★ RETRO DESIGN

The Clifford Pier

Studio Foreign Policy Design Group   *Designer* Yah-Leng Yu, Liquan Liew & Adeline Tan

Sharing an entity with its heritage, The Clifford Pier draws from its legacy as a bustling port in Singapore during the 1930s. The ginger flower motifs pay homage to William Farquhar who was fascinated with local botany during his time on the island. Collaterals with color palette in sea foam, coral and caspian blue; classic postage stamps accented with tropical flora and fauna, along with architectural elements, are reminiscent of the glorious voyages that set sail from this historical landmark.

THE CLIFFORD PIER
SINGAPORE
1933

Hawthorne & Wren Identity

Studio A3 Design | *Designer* Kevin Cantrell

Hawthorne & Wren specialises in producing meaningful gifts of comfort. "Hawthorne" represents honor, respect, hope, and the healing of broken hearts, since hawthorn wood is known for strength and durability, suggesting longevity and endurance. "Wren" acts as the messenger, suggesting the need to share with others a message of hope and optimism, like a song to the heart. Hence, Hawthorne & Wren gives meaning to emotions and wings to words. The colours reinforce the handmade, nature-inspired quality that symbolises life and vitality.

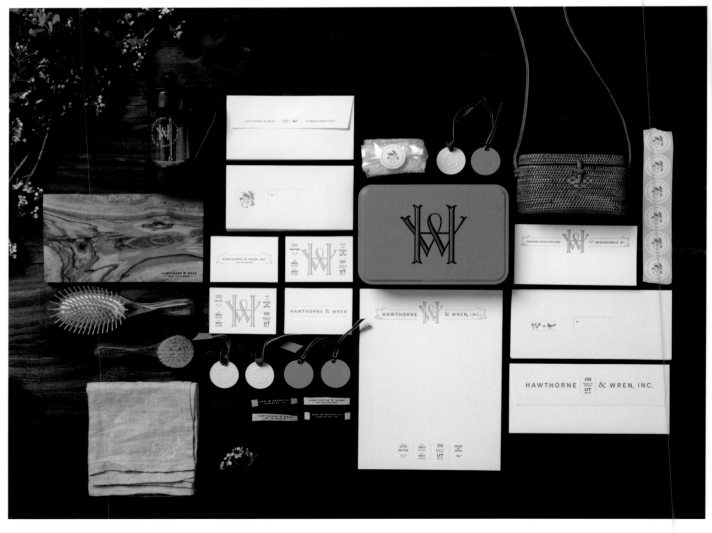

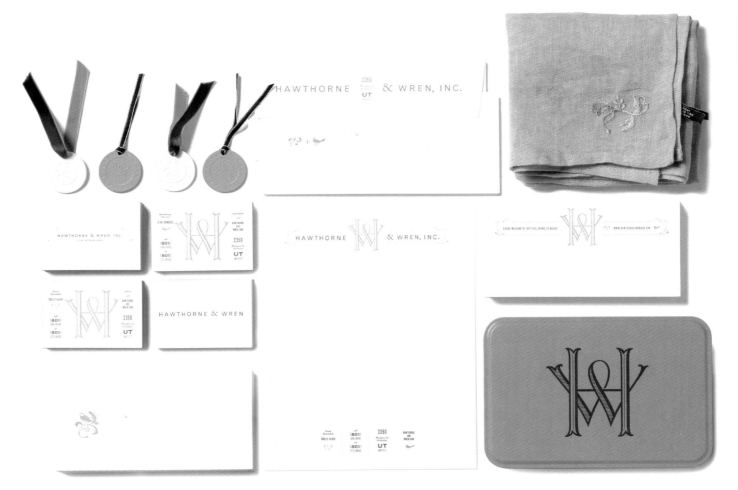

Linnaea

Studio Mash

"Linnaea Rhizotomi" is the first release wine of Linnaea. The founders both have backgrounds in medical anthropology and plant biochemistry. Therefore, a modern yet slightly twisted interpretation of rhizotomy was created, implying life and nature.

Mária Almenara

Studio Wallnut Studio   *Designer* Maria Antonia Echeverry

Mária Almenara has been one of Peru's most established bakery and catering businesses for years. The design draws inspiration from the owner's grandmother's cookbooks, and her nostalgic childhood memories of learning some of the most classic preparations of typical American cuisine, including links to themes like the classic cook Julia Child, lots of old and dusty recipe books, traditional prints found in tablecloths, and the aprons and textiles that could be found in the kitchens of the late 1950s and 1960s.

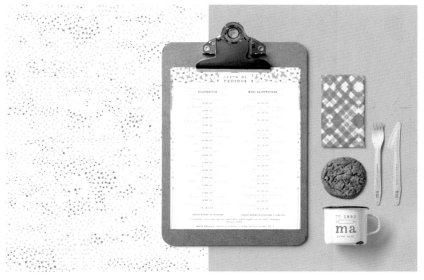

Montagü — Gastro Winebar

Designer Diego Leyva

Montagu is a Spanish-Mexican restaurant in Mexico City. The design take advantage of handmade type and unique illustrations to reflect rare spices and creative dishes Montagu provides, conveying a sense of harmony between ingredients, taste and design.

Moomah Cafe

Studio Apartment One   *Designer* Spencer Bagley & Dean Nicastro

The designers first looked to identify the essence of Moomah and simplified it into four core values: connection, creativity, discovery, and nourishment. They then developed variations of the logo with everyday objects that represented each value. They pushed the boundaries of traditional identity development by extending the brand's identity beyond the logo and name and creating an ownable graphic vernacular that encapsulated the whimsy, wonder, and heart of the brand.

moomah

sip slowly

chill out

stick together

connect

nourish

discover

create

art and nature class

Every semester children explore the natural world through printmaking, collage, sculpting, painting, bookmaking, sewing, felting, storytelling, music, imaginative play, and dance. Each class, the students are introduced to a new topic, given a tutorial with the materials and then offered creative space in which to explore their own unique experience. Something as simple as a leaf rubbing or building a nest can be a wonderful way to help a child connect with nature and the world around them.

full steam ahead

away we go

home sweet home

yummy goodness

Mother India, the Norway's oldest authentic Indian restaurant, was opened in 1993 by the Sharma family. The brand identity was inspired by India's rich culture, from its ancient woodblock printing art which features beautiful ornaments and shapes to India's Bharat Mata meaning Mother India, the national personification of India as a mother goddess. Another source of inspiration was the vintage photos of the country and the Sharma family which were used throughout the identity.

Mother India

Restaurant
India
SPICY
VINDALOO
No.1 रेस्टोरेंट
Tikka masala
Tandoori
Sharma

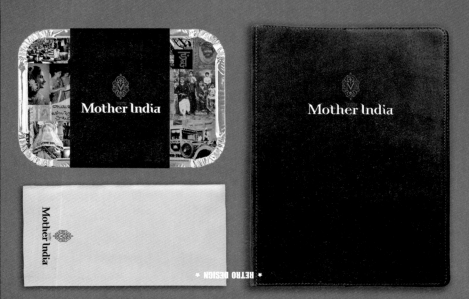

★ RETRO DESIGN ★

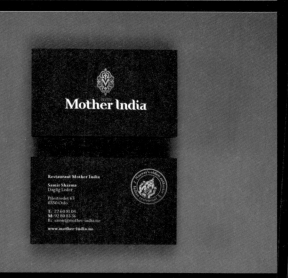

Pelman Hand Made Cafe

Studio G-sign

Pelman is a fast food restaurant of old-school style, which draws inspiration from the 1950s of America but with a modern interpretation. The main character is a brutal middle-aged man with a chic mustache and strong arms in tattoos. His face can be found from coffee cups, bags to crafted to-go boxes.

107

The Vault

Designer Antonio Rodrigues Jr

This project was originally commissioned by a pop/rock band, and developed as a personal project. The images are about grief and confusion. Each faceless character's head is decorated with antelope's horns, looking like hanging trophies.

Treasure Island Music Festival

> **Designer** Johnny Chang

Treasure Island Music Festival held in San Francisco, was named after the novel *Treasure Island* by Robert Louis Stevenson, who lived in San Francisco for a bit of his life. The designer was inspired by the adventures of treasure hunting in this novel and decided to bring that into our modern world. These are the silkscreened posters and collateral for the festival. On the backs of all the printed collateral are pieces of a large treasure map. Attendees of the festival will not only enjoy music, but also get to experience the adventure of treasure hunting during the festival.

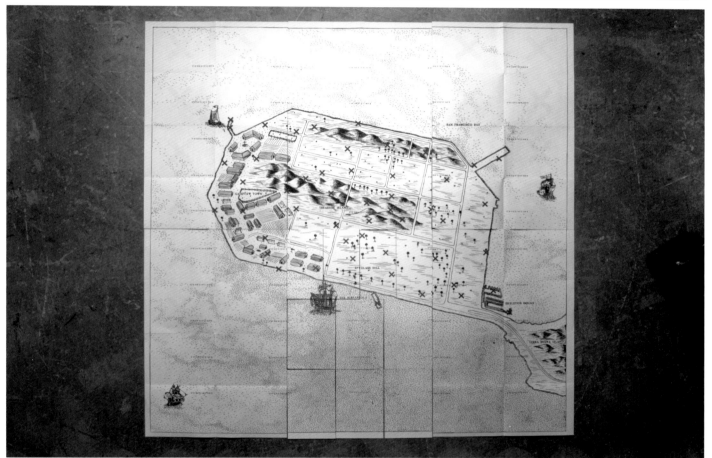

The Rabbit & Monday Misfits

Studio Sciencewerk Design   **Designer** Danis Sie

This is the event branding for Danis & Tiara's wedding. The rabbit mark is inspired from the Chinese zodiac. The illustration drawn by contemporary surrealist artist Roby Dwi Antono tells the story of the couple's 8 years being together.

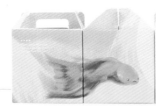

Sommelier Anatoly Markov Identity

Studio Eskimo design studio   *Designer* Emelyanov Pavel

The wooden case serves as a sommelier's wine box. It is marked suitably, including the the alcohol content, bottle volume, and bottling date. A set of seals for imprinting date numbers can be used to decorate the sommelier's business cards.

The Pavlovsky Posad Shawl Museum

Studio Times Branding   *Designer* Valeria Polubiatko

Museum of Russian Shawls is a unique museum situated in Pavlovsky Posad. The museum features a rare collection of shawls from the late 18th to early 20th centuries: campaign shawls, anniversary shawls of the tsar era, and historical shawls. The corporate identity is created by arranging the fragments of shawls into seven layers of kaleidoscopes. The multi-layered patterns symbolize the variety of exhibitions held by the museum.

павлопосадские платки

юбилейные платки

агитационные платки

Fanakalo Studio
South Africa

We love vintage. We love the frills and etchings and shading done in gritty halftone dots and lettering done in what could never ever have been put into a functional typeface of a computer. We love illustrations that were done by hand, misregistration and overprinting of printing techniques, paper that you can feel, and ink that you can smell.

But why? To us it's the nostalgia of that bygone era of "they don't make them like they used to", an era of typesetting by hand that took days in order to create a mere pamphlet. It's layers of detail that we as consumers in today's hustle and bustle rat race will never truly appreciate or spend enough time to take in because we're keeping one eye on that next WhatsApp message or social media post.

We love what we refer to as "retro vintage". We're not fooling anyone into believing that anything we designed was created in the 1930s, 1950s or 1970s. We started branding wine companies as we are based in Stellenbosch, the little epicentre of South Africa's wine industry. Wine brands have their vintage feel in nature. There is no hiding the fact that the label on the bottle was designed in the last five to ten years, but we are definitely using vintage imagery and designs for a reason. They communicate the same passion and vigour as that of those designers decades ago. They not only communicate our passion towards instilling a craftsmanship in the creation of the label's design, but also demonstrate the handcrafted approach and process of making wine. And this is not a Houdini illusion that we as designers are trying to perform in front of consumers' eyes. It sprouts from a direct answer to the market's demand. Form follows function and the current era demands attention to detail. Key words like "artisanal", "hand crafted" and "finely made" have become daily clichés that we build into our current food packaging. The "established in..." date bears weight. And not only packaging for food, carpentry, food markets with focus on the local and the organic, restaurants and clothing are all carving out a segment in which you can now buy the"real deal", made in the "old school" way. The single fin movement of surfing longboards has never been bigger in the last 30 years and the emphasis is not on performance any more. The emphasis is now on style and the decorative elements that goes with it. Netflix has a documentary *Making the American Man* that highlighted how people fought against "Made in China" by making their products by hand.

We still buy our washing powder in the cheapest bulk form possible, but on weekends we want to sip, taste and talk about that naturally fermented, bush vine, Grenache Blanc that was organically or even bio-dynamically grown in a corner of the world where there is no electricity or cell phone reception. At Fanakalo we are but mere slaves to this appreciation of detail when creating a product. And we enjoy it.

Basson Laubscher & The Violent Free Peace

Studio Fanakalo

The Collage of old photos and bold-coloured prints gave a vintage feel to the brand. Visual elements explode from the middle sleeve like notes flowing out of the guitar solo of Basson's vintage Marshall amp. Each song title on the back is captured by its own unique retro icon. The CD disc is made to look like an old Decca vinyl with white printed on black. Basson is one of the old-school blues best performed by using maple guitars and hot valve amps and this album's vintage images are a tribute to that.

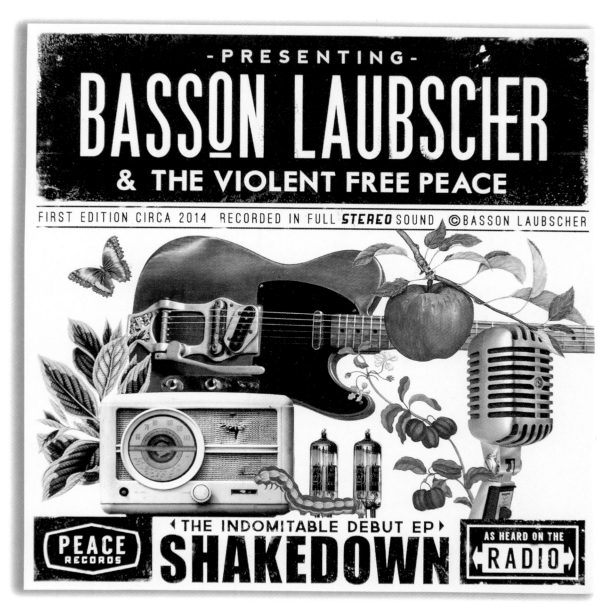

Khulu Soap

Studio Fanakalo

Khulu Soap is an original and authentic manufacturer of soaps and is also the first to launch this type of product in South Africa after two years of experimentation with different combinations of herbs. The handmade soap is infused with traditional wild herbs from the heart of Africa. There are 5 different soaps, each packaged and designed with a specific African theme.

ISIVUTHEVUTHE
for
LOVERS
THEY WILL HAVE EYES FOR ONLY YOU!

KHULU SOAP

FEEL THE POWER OF AFRICA!

THEY WILL ONLY
– HAVE EYES –
FOR YOU!

4.4 oz
(125g)

uBUHLE BENTOMBI
BEAUTY
NATURE'S BEAUTY SECRET

AFRICAN SHEA BUTTER,
UNUKANI, UMKHUHLU, ULOSLINE,
UNGINAKILE, UVUMA OMHLOPE,
INCEMASHELA, INGOBAMAKHOSI

KHULU SOAP

FEEL THE POWER OF AFRICA!

4.4 oz
(125g)

INHLOLI
GOOD LUCK
REMOVES SKIN IMPURITIES
& BAD SPIRITS

BRINGS GOOD LUCK
REMOVES SKIN IMPURITIES
& BAD SPIRITS

KHULU SOAP

FEEL THE POWER OF AFRICA!

4.4 oz
(125g)

UBUHLE BEMVELO
INNER
BEAUTY
FOR BEAUTY
&
GOOD FORTUNE

FOR *Beauty*
& GOOD FORTUNE

KHULU SOAP

FEEL THE POWER OF AFRICA!

4.4 oz
(125g)

Gastropub Albatros

Studio Bureau Bumblebee   *Designer* Igor Khrupin

Gastropub Albatros is a combination of Soviet Russia romance and modern fun. It is an awesome place that will appeal to those who still recall the famous yellow beer barrels on the street and those who heard about them from their parents. Referencing Soviet nostalgia, the branding materials are a nod to the Soviet Union and an appeal to a demographic of young and urban professionals.

Beachy Cream

Studio Design Womb   **Designer** Nicole LaFave

Beachy Cream Ice Cream creates organic ice cream sandwiches, scoops, and cones in Los Angeles, California. The branding winks at surf life and nods at polka dot bikinis. Design Womb successfully designed and delivered a whimsical and vintage-inspired collection of ice cream pint packaging for the brand's signature flavors. The packages have a modern touch on retro, utilizing a bright and creamy color palette with their signature stripes and pin-up girl.

127

Brew No.2 Maple Porter Beer

Studio Craig Valentino Design   *Designer* Craig Valentino

For the 2014 / 2015 holiday season, F & S once again created its annual homebrew to share with friends and family. Full branding was created for this brew, and details like hangtag and a full-length sealing strip gives the packaging a hand-crafted touch. The branding has an overall vintage feel with its color scheme and natural kraft paper, but also a modern touch with the use of clean linework and sans serif fonts.

Bumble Bee Playing Cards

Designer Oban Jones   *Photographer* Peter McKinnon

Inspiration was taken from the romanticized idea of the Victorian bee keeper in his cottage, a simple man living in sync with his surroundings. The design feels as though the bee keeper has fashioned the deck himself for sunny games of solitaire overlooking his thriving hives. These were designed with the Ellusionist Playing Card Company to help raise support and awareness for the dwindling bee population.

Father's Day Card

Designer Giada Tamborrino

This Father's Day card has been designed with the idea of representing tradition and everlasting love in the modern age. With a vintage but fresh twist, it has been printed on kraft paper to give it a retro feeling not only to the eye but also to the touch.

HAPPY

father's

DAY

Golden Heritage of the Scythians

Designer Alexey Seoev

The samogon "Golden Heritage of the Scythians" is produced on the territory of the motherland of the Don Cossacks — the land that once belonged to the tribes of powerful Scythians — and made according to the special recipe without purification. The drink is the product of superb quality and contains gold leaves of unmatched purity. The Scythian deer is one of the most famous images for the gold jewelry, found by archeologists in the ancient mounds as a symbolic representation of Scythians "animal style". This symbol is the key element of the label.

Bières du château

Studio A3 Studio   *Designer* Yvo Hählen & Priscilla Balmer

Based in Lausanne, Switzerland, Brasserie Artisanale du Château commissioned graphic design A3 Studio to create four new labels for their traditionally made beer, as well as a new four-pack packaging. The labels are inspired by the sea world and are decorated with ropes. The illustrations (a whale, a corset, a siren, and a ship) are drawn by hand to emphasize the handmade production of the beer. They are inspired by old engraving and sailors' tattoos. Printed on kraft paper, the labels stress the authenticity of the beer. The brown cardboard of the 4-pack completes the look.

137

Dian & Wicak Wedding Invitation

Designer Diasty Hardhikaputri

In Indonesia, wedding is not just a "knot" tied between two persons. In relation to that, the invitation for this wedding is designed with unique pop-up decorations to accommodate the information about the wedding plus the photo of the couple. Finished with the application of gold and silver elements into design, the invitation shows reflection of luxury with intense personality to the overall concept. The notebook becomes a memorable wedding gift because of its unique design that resembles cookies, showcasing the couple's heartfelt passion towards the culinary world, especially their love for baking.

Brooklyn Wedding Invitations

Designer Alicia Pompei & Rosalind Roongseang

The letterpress wedding invitations featured an oak tree illustration as their focal point to represent the setting for the nuptials, inside New York's Brooklyn Park.

9 Questions

Studio Until Sunday   *Designer* Chiara Aliotta

It is a promotional gift for Christmas sent by Boutique Creativa, a communication design studio, to all their clients. Until Sunday came up with a board game that answers their clients' most common question: "Which is the right creative agency for my new project?" The game includes 9 cards, 4 pawns and 2 dices. Each spot tells an interesting or historic fact about the history of graphic design. The 9 Questions logo is the number 9 "dressed" like a joker.

Caro — Vital Album Art

Designer Hsiao-Ron Cheng

Using digital painting, this project is the illustration and design for Imaginary Flower, the vinyl release of Caro, a singer from Austin, Texas in the USA. Beautiful pastel colours bestow the design with a sense of elegance and romance.

Side A / Imaginary Flower
Side B / Abyss

Written by *Carolyn Somes*
Produced by *Stephen Doster*
Lead Vocals & Guitar - *Carolyn Somes*
Guitar - *Stephen Doster*
Bass - *Felipe Archer*
Drums - *Dony Wynn*
Rhodes - *Mandy Rowden*
Sitar - *Pablo Escalante*
Backing Vocals - *Baylee Kuss*
Recorded and Mixed by *James Stevens*
at EAR Studio in Austin, TX

Casa Gusto Packaging

Studio The Creative Method   *Designer* Tony Ibbotson & Mayra Monobe

The Casa Gusto packaging takes its roots from the Italian Circus in the 1950s when the owner's father used to travel the country following the circus and sampling the best ingredients. The illustrations are really distinctive, as they reflect the individual personality of the circus staff. The packaging is bold, bright and attracts immediate attention in the very bland business of bulk food selling.

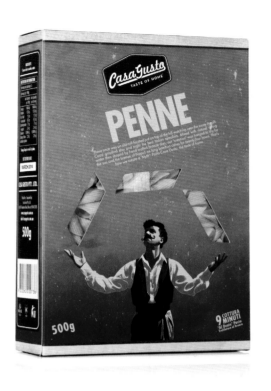

Cristina & David Wedding Invitation

Studio El Calotipo Printing Studio   *Designer* Nelson Moya & Carla Nicolás

These are the wedding invitations of Cristina and David. Inspired by the place where the wedding was going to be celebrated: the Pyrenees, the designer tried to make them have certain similarity with such a fabulous settlement, playing with wild motives and using materials to provide some warmth. He used cardboard as the main material and decorated the invitations with artisanal seal and a piece of a cord. The cord would keep the invitation and the plan hidden, preventing the attendees from getting lost at all important places of celebration.

Cristina
&David
13 de julio de 2013

Nos casamos

Os esperamos
a las 17:30 h. el **13 de julio** de 2013.
en la **Iglesia Parroquial de San Pedro**

Viridian Hats Party

Studio tegusu   *Designer* Masaomi Fujita

This is designed for "Hats Party", an event held at the custom hats shop Viridian on August 10th, 2013. August 10th is designated as "Hats Day" in the hat industry in Japan. The designer created a gentleman's face using the numbers 8, 1 and 0 as a mascot for this event. He also designed pin badges and bookmarks using typography as gifts to the guests and set the mood for the party.

Cinemaas

Studio byRosa   Designer Rosa de Jong

These were business cards made for Dutch director Danny Maas, director of commercials, video clips and more. The cards were made to look like an old movie stub, and were printed on a real old fashion tickets roll.

Hôtel Excelsior Latin

Studio Mr cup   *Designer* Fabien Barral

Hôtel Excelsior Latin will certainly charm you with his "belle époque" of the beginning of the 20th century Paris and a mixture of modernity and authenticity. In addition, pictures from the 1920s and an old version of the logo hand drawn in 1952 match with the spirit of the hotel's history.

Funny Cabany Grill House

Studio G-sign *Designer* Alina Pimkina & Ilya Kiselev

Funny Cabany is the perfect place for carnivores to congregate. The industrial-chic yet romantic interior decor complements the extensive barbecue and grill menu, which features everything from homemade sausages to deliciously tender steaks.

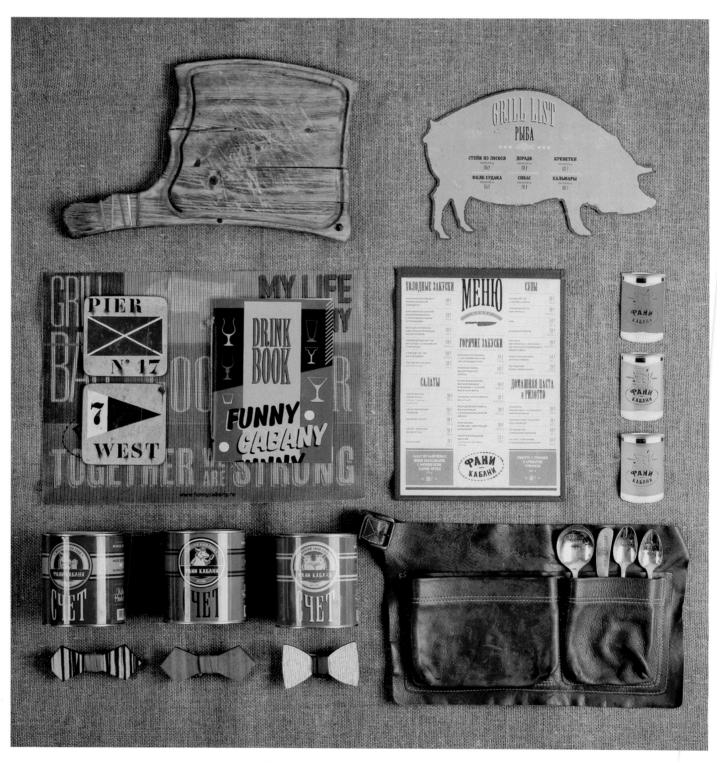

Les Indiennes Texstyles

Studio   H-57 Creative Station

Les Indiennes Texstyles is an atelier based in Milan. For the shoe box packaging, H-57 created a cylindrical box, decorated with the trademark graphics, together with funny and witty suggestions dedicated to women, so as to be stylistically reminiscent of skillful craftsmanship.

Las Buenas Maneras

Studio Wallnut Studio   *Designer* Cristina Londoño

Inspired by antique ceramics and the concept of dinning etiquette, Las Buenas Maneras comes to life by the use of just a blue rollerball pen and some water colours. Vintage spoons and traditional plates combined with tips of table manners are presented across the packaging material and stationery. Rubber stamps with the logotype have also been incorporated to give a handmade rusty final look.

Lost Melody Soap

Designer   Gogo Hiu Ying Chan

In order to give users an unforgettable and meaningful bathing experience, the designer incorporated the music rest notes in her work. To make the notes cohesive with the text, she did hand-lettering for the logo. Besides, water color as a medium was used because its expressiveness and transparency fit the voice for the emotional female customers. To further convey the message of the lost singing habit of girls when they grow up and the idea that girls like hiding their inner side, the designer used vellum paper for the soap label and made the glass bottle frosted.

Lurpak

Studio Pearlfisher

Stemming from the design idea "deliciously authentic", Pearlfisher created a distinctive identity, structure, parchment and outer wrap that celebrated the new slow churned butter in a novel way. The design of this innovative and fully recyclable brushed aluminum butter dish has elevated the specialness of the brand in the Lurpak family, balancing its heritage alongside this new product's artisan and premium positioning.

★ RETRO DESIGN ★

161

Marou Faiseurs de Chocolat

Studio Rice Creative   *Designer* Chi-An De Leo & Joshua Breidenbach

Marou Faiseurs de Chocolat is the first manufacturer to create single origin gourmet bean-to-bar chocolate in Vietnam. Since each flavor corresponds to different provinces from where the cacao beans grow, designers ascribed a natural color shift to different flavors. To highlight the artisanal quality of the brand, traditional silk-screen printing techniques were used with antique gold ink on each wrapper.

Marou for La Grande Épicerie de Paris

Studio   Rice Creative   *Designer*   Chi-An De Leo & Joshua Breidenbach

Marou Faiseurs de Chocolat were approached by La Grande Épicerie de Paris to create an exclusive chocolate bar specifically for their shelves. The building of La Grande Épicerie de Paris were hand drawn in the wrappers, together with geometric pattern and retro fronts, to highlight a 19th century feel.

Marou Treasure Island

Studio Rice Creative   **Designer** Chi-An De Leo & Joshua Breidenbach

Marou Chocolate hand selected the finest cacao beans grown on small family-owned farms on the remote island of Tan Phu Dong, stretching from the two northernmost arms of the Mekong Delta all the way into the sea. To convey the spirit of discovery and rarity, the approach to the packaging adopted was to maintain the primary elements of the brand, but introduce a different, more adventurous graphic language with a vintage map of the area and drawn calligraphy.

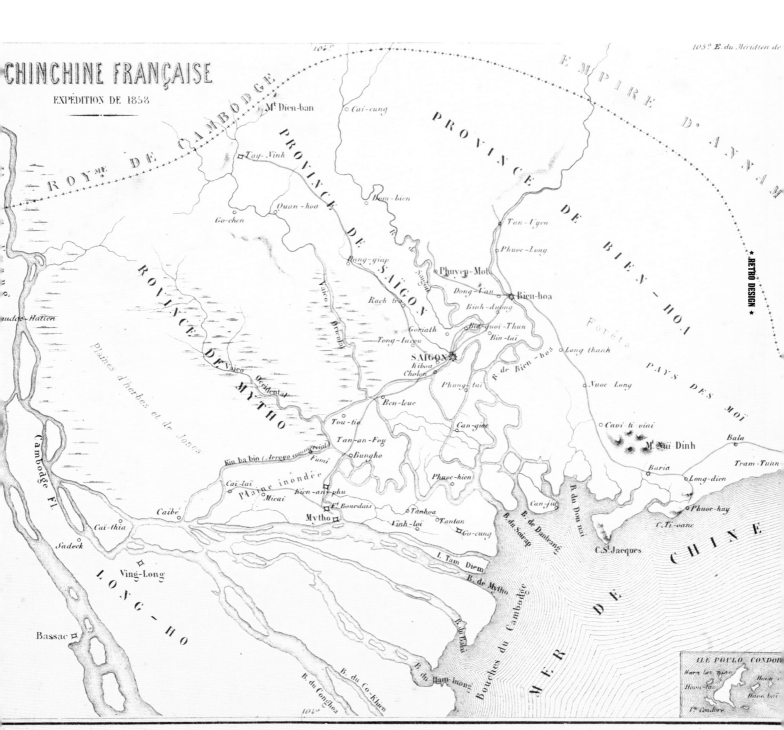

COCHINCHINE FRANÇAISE
EXPÉDITION DE 1858

ROY.ᵐᵉ DE CAMBODGE

EMPIRE D'ANNAM

104°

103° E. du Méridien de

★ RETRO DESIGN ★

Mᵗ Dien-ban
Cai-cung

PROVINCE DE BIEN-HOA

Tay-Vinh

PROVINCE DE SAÏGON

Ouan-hoa
Bam-bien
Go-chen

Tan-Uyen
Phuoc-Long

Rang-giap
Saigon
Phuyen-Mot

PROVINCE DE MYTHO

Vaico Oriental

Dong-Van
Bien-hoa

Rach-tra

Binh-duong

Goriath
But-quoi-Thun

Tong-Iacou
Bin-tai

SAÏGON
Riboa
Cholon

R. de Bien-hoa

Long-thanh

Forêts

PAYS DES Moi

P'hung-tai
Nuoc-Long

Vaico Occidental

Ben-leuc

Cavi-ti-viai

Tou-tia
Can-giac

Mᵗ Nui Dinh
Bala

Tan-an-Fou

Plaines d'herbes et de Jones

Kin-ba-bio (Arroyo commercial)

Fumi
Bungho

Phuoc-hien

Tram-Tuan

Baria

Long-dien

Cai-lai
kien-anr-phu

Plaine inondée

Micai

Eᵗ Bourdais

Tanhoa

Can-jir

B. du Don-nai

Phuoc-kay

C. Ti-oane

Cambodge Fl.

Caibé

Mytho

Vinh-loi
Fantan

R. du Soirap

B. de Dantrang

C. S.ᵗ Jacques

Cai-thia

Go-cung

Sadeck

I. Tam-Diem

MER DE CHINE

LONG-HO
Ving-Long

B. de Mytho

Bassac

Bouches du Cambodge

B. du Co-Khen
B. du Conghoa

B. du Ham-inong

104°

ÎLE POULO-CONDOR

reau

Furne, Jouvet et Cⁱᵉ éditeurs

165

Mercado 1143

Studio Mola Ativism **Designer** Rui Morais

The year of the foundation of Portugal led the designer to the creation of Mercado 1143 (Market 1143), a brand that features a coat of arms and a timeless seal of warranty. It is linked to the popular tone of communication suitable to those taverns and markets.

TEMOS PROVAS QUE SER PORTUGUÊS TEM VALOR

DE MERCADO

DESCUBRA-O, BREVEMENTE, À NOSSA MESA

Noble Petite Packaging

Studio Heather Nguyen Design   *Designer* Heather Nguyen

Noble Handcrafted is a brand that embraces the collaboration of craft with the new American food tradition. Noble Petite is inspired by the jewelry from the early 1900s. The designer loved the ornate decorative elements, which spoke of craftsmanship and elegance, and used black-and-white printing on uncoated, cream textural paper to tie it back to the Noble Handcrafted brand.

Shiraz & Sehresh Wedding Invitation

Designer Shiraz Malik

The design revolves around the bride and groom's conflicting personalities and backgrounds. Sehresh Malik is a person of a traditional perspective while Shiraz Malik, the groom and designer comes from a modern and easy-going family, finding his voice in the retro feel and vintage impressions. By keeping their backgrounds in mind, a retro kitsch style was developed to enhance the overall locomotion and propulsion of a Pakistani wedding.

PAZ (TE)

Designer Danielle Orkin

The project aims to create a Spanish tea brand that can evoke a peaceful, Mediterranean feel. The proposal consists of 4 printed boxes. The prints on the boxes are interchangeable and they work well together in creating a strong shelf appeal. The typography has been inspired by Spanish street graffiti and signage. Each tea bag packaging was printed with quotes about peace.

Monica Corporate Identity

Studio We meet Brands   *Designer* Roberta Farese

This is the visual and corporate identity for a new Italian fashion label called Monica. The beautiful floral pattern, the typography, and the emblem work harmoniously to lend an elegant and vintage feel to the design.

LIMITED EDITION

·BY·
MONICA
FOR
CRONULLA
№07 ROMA 129⅞

Monster Chocolate Co.

Designer Robin L. Short

Monster Chocolate Co. is a conceptual line of novelty chocolate products that would ideally be found in curiosity shops and specialty food stores. With a love for the Victorian era, the designer wanted to find what could be fascinating, mysterious, and beautiful all at once. The Victorian-inspired patterns are all hand illustrated and the metallic gold paper offers a luxurious feeling for a truly unique chocolate brand.

MONSTER
CHOCOLATE CO.
MADE IN Coney Island, NY

The Bohemian Twins! In 1910, Rosa Blazer (and her sister Josepha) was denied marriage to the father of her son by the French court because it was considered bigamy.

Nutrition Facts
Serv. Size 1.4 oz
Servings 1

Fat Cal. 130

%DV*
20%
46%
1%
6%

MONSTER
CHOCOLATE CO.
DOUBLE DARK
CHOCOLATE & CACAO NIBS
70% CACAO

MONSTER
CHOCOLATE CO.
MEXICAN AN
DIPPING CHOC

MONSTER
CHOCOLATE CO.
LAVENDER DARK
DARK SIPPING CHOCOLATE
60% CACAO

MONSTER
CHOCOLATE CO.
HAZELNUT
CHOCOLATE SPREAD

Ronner

Studio Wallnut Studio **Designer** Maria Antonia Echeverry

Ronner is a sophisticated and established clothing brand created for the equestrian market in both North and South America. A rich packaging system was created with a strong sense of English elegance. Soft paper, high quality Provencal textiles and added touches of gold in the printing process finish the look of the brand.

181

Sauce Restaurant

Studio Marty Weiss and Friends   **Designer** Eulie Lee

Sauce is Chef Frank Prisinzano's 4th restaurant. To be consistent with the style of Frank's other restaurants, the identity is featured with grandmotherly wallpapers. The typography was inspired by the old New York Italian Pork and Grocery storefronts.

78-84 *Rivington* STREET
NEW YORK, NY 10002

212.420.7700

SAUCERESTAURANT.COM

SAYEGUSA 145th Anniversary

Studio Keiko Akatsuka & Associates   *Designer* Keiko Akatsuka

SAYEGUSA is a long-established children clothing store at Ginza, Tokyo. To celebrate its 145th anniversary, an invitation card was designed to resemble a shopfront full of girl's romantic imagination.

Shiseido Benefique

Studio Studio Tord Boontje **Designer** Tord Boontje

For the relaunch of the Benefique range of cosmetics in Japan, the designer developed packaging artwork taking inspiration from nature. Endangered plants can be discovered alongside animals, birds, and butterflies. This was applied to both the product and the outer packaging.

187

Staropramen Limited Edition Cans

Studio BBDO Ukraine   **Designer** Martynas Birskys & Konstantin Kondrashin

In April, 2014, SUN InBev Ukraine and BBDO Ukraine presented a special limited line of cans to the true fans of Czech beer Staropramen. Each of four unique cans represents one of Charles Bridge, the iconic building of Czech. Each medieval statue on the bridge can tell one of the many legends associated with this place.

Staropramen 2015

Studio BBDO Ukraine ***Designer*** Mariya Teterina, Konstantin Kondrashin & Martynas Birskys

The core value of Staropramen 2015 series lies in Prague the city itself: its versatility, ancient streets and glorious architectures. The designers have made a journey through the ages and architecture that influenced the face of Prague, and implemented it into the limited edition can series, which were emphasized by authentic legends on the back.

★ RETRO DESIGN ★

Teasy

Studio Coba&associates   **Designer** Vesna Pešić BECHA

Teasy is an instant tea brand offering tea bags of several flavours. Its use of traditional ingredients is conveyed through those retro illustrations of Victorian characters. To appeal to young generation, the packaging was incorporated with a sense of modern style, making it both classic and trendy.

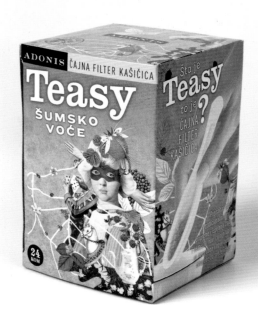

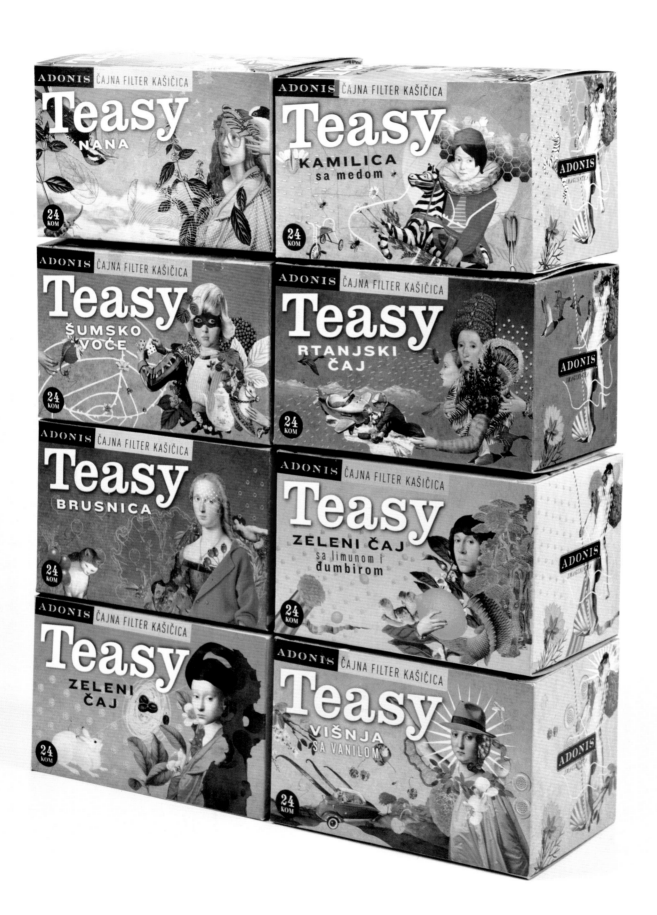

The Jane Austen Book Boutique

Studio KITA Designs   **Designer** Nikita Gill

The Jane Austen Book Boutique is a tiny corner store in Jane Austen's town, specializing in Austen style literature, amongst other feminine and feminist driven literature. The designer used a simple font coupled with Jane Austen's own signature to create a memorable look for the store and chose soft, feminine colours together with a delicate pattern for the project.

Thomas J. Fudge's

Studio big fish *Designer* Victoria Sawdon

Fudges is a Dorset-based family bakery opened for almost 100 years. Faced with a lot of competition from supermarket-own brands, the brand asked big fish to re-position them to their rightful place as the finest biscuits available and changed their name from Fudges to Thomas J. Fudge's Remarkable Bakery. The designer illustrated the packs with eccentric Victorian imagery, including beautiful drawings of plants and flowers to emphasize the product ingredients and flavors, and finished them with vibrant splashes of color.

MANY-SHAPED MISCELLANY
OF BISCUITS FOR CHEESE

AN INDISPENSABLE SELECTION OF SAVOURY BITES FOR
CHEESE TASTING, SUPPERS AND WINE SIPPING SESSIONS

300G
10.5oz℮

Evil Spirits Vodka

Studio St. Bernadine   *Designer* Jennifer Hicks

Evil Spirits is a new premium spirits line that is painstakingly crafted to be sinfully enjoyed. The design team extended the brand promise of "evil" through every detail of the design language, such as custom word mark, spirit renderings in matte varnish, recipe card and Ouija board with commemorative cast pewter planchette.

Gladio

Studio Flat Design Studio *Designer* Max Lippolis

Gladio an Italian high energy drink. To attract the customers and to stand out from the numerous other beverages the designer based the main concept on the Roman gladiator by incorporating the helmet element. The dark light symbolises the occurrence of strength, whereas the red side stands for ancient Romans and blood colour.

★ RETRO DESIGN ★

Wimbledon & Make-A-Wish

Studio Paula Peters Design   *Designer* Paula Peters

This piece is an event invite to the pre-party at the Wimbledon Tennis Championships. The invitation contains a double-sided poster that wraps around the actual invite and R.S.V.P. It is hoped that those invited would keep this piece as a memento or reminder of the event and over-time, the piece would eventually become a collected and treasured series. The invite itself includes a custom die-cut of the logo and hand-rendered watercolour illustrations.

The Muddy Basin Ramblers — Formosa Medicine Show CD

Studio Onion Design Associates   *Designer* Andrew Wong & Fong Ming Yang

The Muddy Basin Ramblers is a jug band from Taipei. They play music from the turn of the century such as old time Jazz, blues and ragtime. This is also a concept album based on medicine show from the 1920s. So the graphic style tries to authentically represent the period of the history. The physical copy of "Formosa Medicine Show" is wrapped in a 45-RPM record sleeve and printed on vintage newspaper-style broadsheets.

The Original Savory

Studio Serious Studio

The Original Savory , first opened in the 1950s, is one of the oldest restaurant chains in the Philippines. The design of their print materials were derived from the vintage aesthetic of Old Manila. The designers created various posters reminiscent of advertisements and print materials in the 1950s and then applied them onto the space. The restaurant features a mural of vintage-inspired posters and a gallery that contains snippets of the brand's history and traditions, which transport diners to the look and feel of that era.

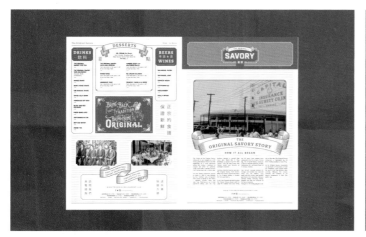

203

E-g-sain 2014 Chinese New Year

Studio MURA Design *Designer* Tom Chen, Ssu Ying Pan & Oli Syu

The Spring Festival (Chinese Lunar New Year) is a unique festival for the Chinese, with different zodiacs symbolising different auspicious meanings; all these denoted meanings are heritage from the previous dynasties in China's history. From the ancient Chinese way of calculating the astrological facts in the calendar, the designers produce graphics and colour system for the package in "Golden Horse" year. According to different products' qualities, different packages tell different stories. "Dancing Horse" from China's Tang Dynasty is a lucky symbol for happiness and peace during the Spring Festival.

Golden Eagle Handmade Suit

Designer Miao-Ting Jhu & Yi-Chun Chen

Handmade suit is the witness of modern Chinese history as well as the spirit of master craftsmen, who create the unique and graceful bearing of handmade suit by sewing each stitch. Golden Eagle is a series of books about the traditional handmade suit industry in Taiwan. Due to the big change of times and the decline of the industry, the designers decided to use what they have learned in school to let the public know more about handmade suit and explore the beauty of handwork.

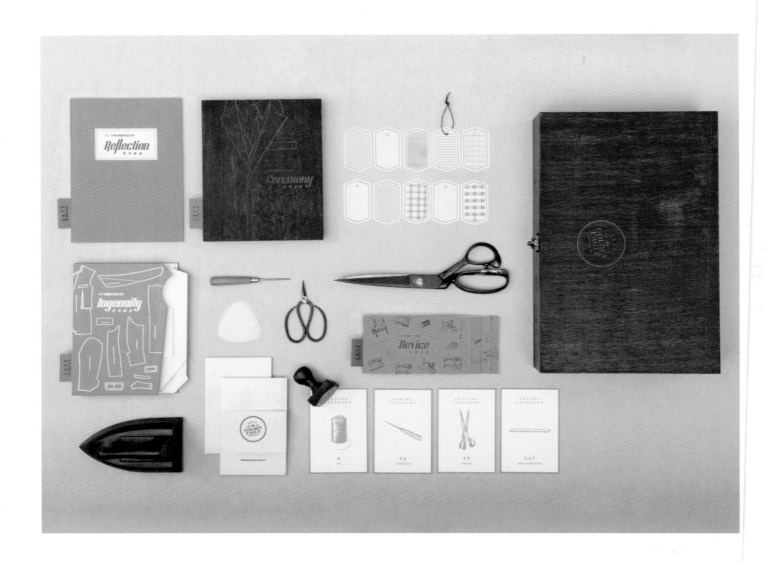

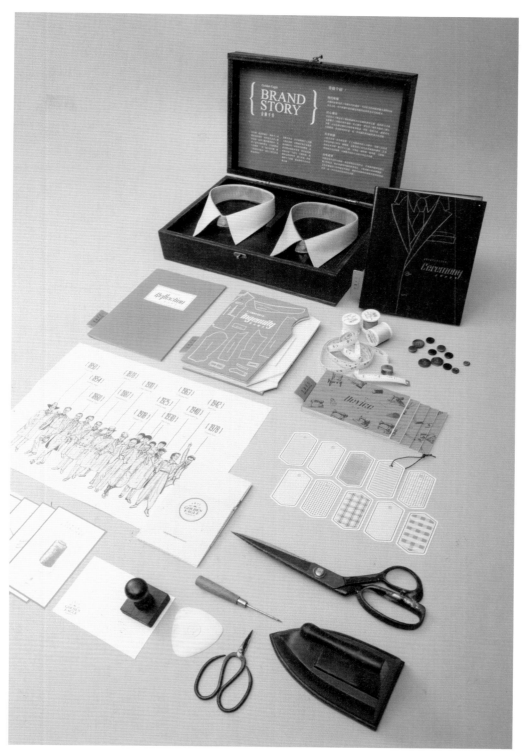

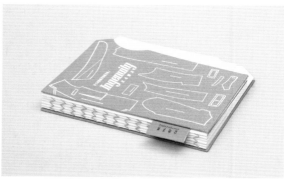

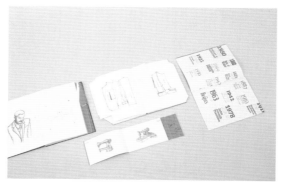

38 Mitsubachi Hachimitsu

Studio ANONIWA   *Designer* Naoto Kitaguchi

This packaging is for a new range of products released by a railway company. Ever since it was founded, the railway has carried passengers reliably day in and day out, just as bees carefully carry nectar from flowers back to the hive. This abstract connection between bees and railway rail led to the creation of a logo that communicates the commitment of the railway company to its passengers, a commitment which has remained unchanged ever since the first train departed.

Mira Moon Hotel

Studio Miramar Group *Designer* Alex Lau & Angel Tsang

Drawing inspiration from the Moon Festival fairytale that tucks at the public's heartstrings, Jade Rabbit and the moon are the key elements for Mira Moon's style-savvy brand identity. Chinese patterns and the peony flower are nods to tradition while the primary colours of red, black and white imbue the brand collaterals with modernity. The boutique hotel's oriental brand identity mirrors its charming décor and strikes a delicate balance between the old and the new.

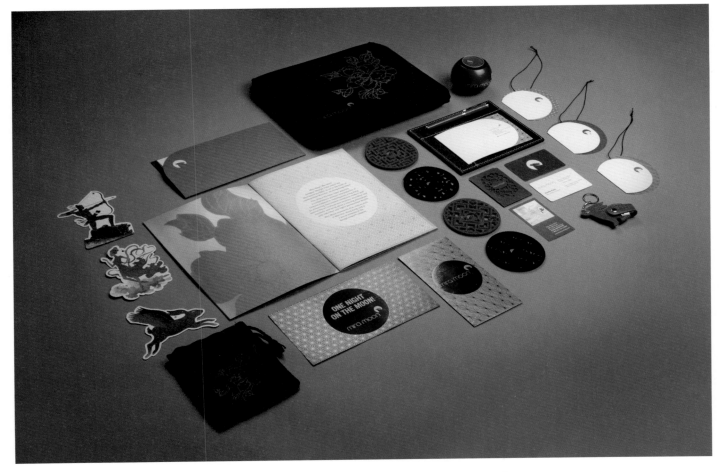

House of Joyful Celebrations Gift Box

Studio Eminent Creative   **Designer** Paggie Chin & Nicole Teh   **Illustrator** YH Loon

The inspiration behind the House of Joyful Celebrations gift box came from the nostalgic days of colonial Malaysian Chinese festive celebrations. Designed to look like an olden day flat complex, the illustration depicts friends and family celebrating Chinese New Year in a variety of joyful ways — from having dinner together to participating in a dragon's dance. Amongst all those smiling faces and memorable moments, there is a feeling of togetherness and reunion, which is the essence of Chinese New Year.

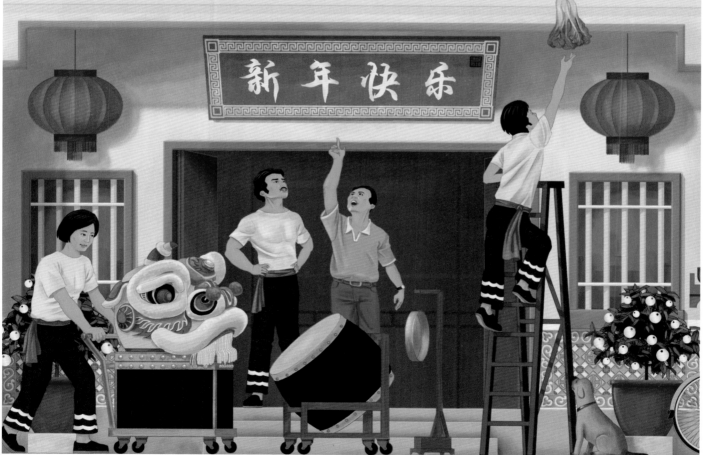

Daebeté Scented Tea

Studio   Victor Branding Design Corp.

The packaging for Daebeté's floral infused oolong tea range, was inspired by the natural beauty and ecology of the flowers' growing regions. The natural beauty and ecology is effectively delivered through an illustrative approach that mixes a variety of flowers and insects such as dragonfly, butterfly, ladybug and bee. There is a great contrast between the lightness of the flowers and the dark leaves. An appropriate use of water color emphasizes the hand painted sensibilities of each illustration and reflects both the craft of tea making and natural flavor.

GUO GUAN — China Classics Collection

> **_Designer_** Penny Peng <

Guo Guan is a brand of traditional Chinese white wine, which is served in important official or business occasions as an upscale wine genre. To represent Chinese elements, the designer chose a scroll structure which is used as traditional book-binding to distinguish itself from other rival brands. On the wine package, traditional Chinese paintings and calligraphies of cloisonné colours are added to stress the brand's market orientation on elite consumers.

Xin Yue Herbal Tea

◁ *Designer* Peng Chao ▷

The packaging illustrations were based on the various ingredients of herbal tea. The use of flowers, birds, etc.—the unique symbols of Chinese culture is delicately integrated with the elegant colours, bringing vividness and freshness to the overall design. Besides, the colours of the smaller packages are different from each other, yet organized in a way that constitutes a system of gradient colours, making the design even more unique, colourful yet unified overall.

INDEX

INDEX

ACKNOWLEDGEMENTS

We would like to thank all the designers and contributors who have been involved in the production of this book; their contributions have been indispensable to its creation. We would also like to express our gratitude to all the producers for their invaluable opinions and assistance throughout this project. And to the many others whose names are not credited but have made helpful suggestions, we thank you for your continuous support.

FUTURE PARTNERSHIPS

If you wish to participate in SendPoints' future projects and publications, please send your website or portfolio to editor01@sendpoints.cn.